THE
BOOK OF
LOVE

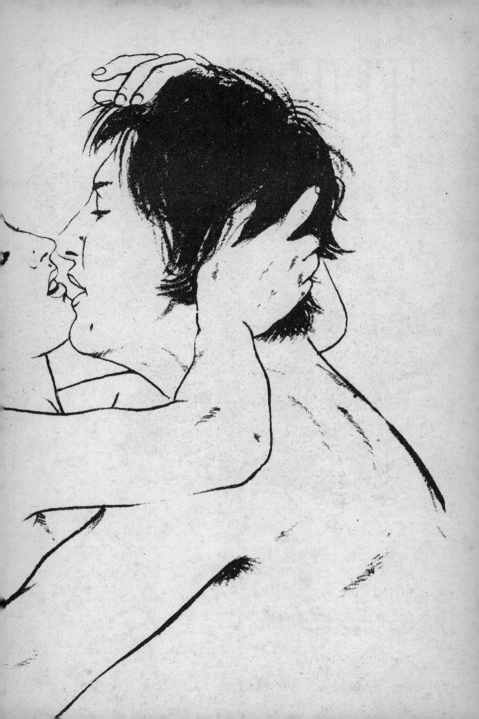

THE BOOK

By this author and published by
New English Library:

THE BOOK OF LOVE
CAREFREE LOVE
HOW TO IMPROVE YOUR SEX LIFE

OF
LOVE
DR. DAVID DELVIN

The Home Doctor Book of Sex and Marriage

Illustrations by Patricia Quayle and Ray Feibush

New English Library in association with MFU Publications

First published in Great Britain by New English Library Ltd 1974
Copyright © 1974 by Dr David Delvin

First NEL Paperback Edition November 1974
Reprinted April 1979
Reprinted March 1980
Reprinted March 1981
Reprinted December 1982
Reprinted October 1983
Reprinted April 1985

*NEL Books are published by New English Library, Mill Road, Dunton Green,
Sevenoaks, Kent. Editorial office: 47 Bedford Square, London WC1B 3DP.
Made and printed in Great Britain by Collins, Glasgow.*

0 450 02320 6

CONTENTS

THE
BOOK OF
LOVE

INTRODUCTION

Despite all the brave talk of a permissive society, the sad fact is that the world is still shrouded in a fog of sexual ignorance, as any doctor working in family planning or related fields will confirm. The distinguished American researchers Masters and Johnson (to whom anyone writing a book of this sort must acknowledge an enormous debt) estimate that serious sexual problems affect perhaps 50% of American marriages, and recent studies suggest that the figures in Britain are not so very different.

Even affluent, well-educated adults are almost laughably misinformed about many aspects of marriage and contraception. Among teenagers and the socially deprived, the depth of ignorance that exists about sexual matters is truly abysmal. It's hardly surprising that countless marriages break up, that VD is rampant, and that pregnancy after pregnancy ends in abortion.

So, this book makes an attempt to dispel at least some of the mists of doubt, misinformation and shame. It's intended to give married and unmarried people the basic facts of sex in a clear, straightforward way, to tell them how to enjoy intercourse, to teach them technique of love-play, to explain all the methods of contraception currently available, to tell them how to deal with sexual problems and common infections of the sex organs, and to provide up-to-date and helpful information about pregnancy and abortion.

The drawings that accompany the text are frank and honest—as they need to be to prevent misunderstanding.

I sincerely hope that those who read the book will find their love-making much safer, much more satisfying—and of course much more fun!

THE
BOOK OF
LOVE

CHAPTER ONE
How a Man is Made

Length of Penis

To the average man, his penis is, consciously or subconsciously, the most important thing in the whole world. At an early age he discovers it and immediately becomes fascinated by it. Soon he notices that little girls are not like him—which usually makes him even prouder of his new-found possession!

But then a note of uncertainty enters his mind. Isn't his really rather small? Look at his Dad's; look at his big brother's; look at those he sees in the changing room at the swimming bath, and he asks himself if he will ever have a whopper like that.

And so he goes on through life, always a tiny bit sensitive about the size of his organ, always convinced that it would be nicer if it were just that little bit longer. No matter how often textbooks repeat that penile size doesn't matter and that women aren't attracted to a man because of the length of his organ, the average male continues to think the same way. It's a fair bet that a high proportion of the male readers of this chapter will by now be eagerly (or anxiously) getting ready to turn the page and thinking to themselves: 'Well, how long does he say it should be then?'

On the other hand, the average female reader is probably amused or amazed at the sheer folly of men in being so obsessed with their penile measurements. Forgive us, ladies—and if you feel tempted to laugh, remember the equally extraordinary obsession that many twentieth century women have with the size of their breasts! As a female, the one thing you need to bear in mind about this ludicrous male preoccupation is this: when in bed with a man, never belittle his penis (even in jest) or say anything to indicate that you think it's small—the poor chap may take you seriously and if he does he'll be deeply hurt. Indeed, I've known of many men whose sensitivity about their penises was such that they actually became impotent after someone had made an unthinking remark about their dimensions.

Now the ridiculous thing about all this was that each of these men had a perfectly normal male organ. Each one just thought he was very small compared with other men. You see, the trouble is that every man sees his own phallus in a foreshortened view— the angle at which he looks down at it inevitably makes it seem shorter than it is. Of course, when he glances at another man's organ in a changing room, there's no such foreshortening effect, so very often it'll look as though the other chap is slightly better endowed than him. A lifetime of comparisons of this sort (and virtually every male does a quick mental check on each naked man he comes across) can very easily make a fellow feel a bit inadequate.

The remedy is twofold. Firstly, anyone who's a bit dissatisfied with the size of his penis (and that probably covers at least 80% of the male readers of this book) should have a good look at it in a mirror now and again; there's no foreshortening in a side view in a looking glass, so he should be relieved by what he sees. It's quite good for the ego (as well as for one's love life generally) to have a large mirror in the bedroom, somewhere fairly adjacent to the bed! There is a pleasant London restaurant of my acquaintance where the management have thoughtfully placed a large mirror in the gents in such a position that the patrons can view themselves side-on while making use of the facilities. By the expressions on their faces, many of them are obviously delighted at the favourable impression of their dimensions that this view gives them.

Secondly, it's important for a man to realise the true facts about the length of a penis. When it is in a non-erect condition (when it's 'flaccid', to use the medical term) the male organ usually measures between 8.5cm. (just over 3″) and 10.5cm. (just over 4″) from tip to base. The average figure is about 9.5cm. (or 3¾″), but this kind of precise measurement is really rather valueless because so many factors (for instance, cold weather or going swimming) can temporarily cause a shrinkage of an inch or more. So all you male readers who've just reached for a tape measure needn't be worried if you happen to fall short of the magic figure of 3¾″.

Of course it's true that some men have big penises and some have small ones, just as some have small and some have big feet, but the measurement is not—repeat *not*—an index of virility. By and large, a flaccid penis is big or small largely because of the degree to which its veins and other blood vessels are open or shut. This physiological factor has nothing to do with hormone levels or any other index of maleness.

Furthermore, the size of the penis does not correlate with the size of a man's body. Most people imagine that a tall, husky man will usually have a large penis, but this is not so at all. The distinguished American researchers Masters and Johnson (who have done so much to increase our knowledge in the field of sex) measured the penile lengths of over 300 men. The largest organ (measuring 14cm., or 5½″, in the flaccid state) belonged to a slim man who was only 5′ 7″ tall; the smallest (measuring 6cm., or 2¼″) belonged to a fairly heavily built man of 5′ 11″.

It's also worth pointing out that there is no correlation between penile size and race. Psychologists believe that a good deal of racial prejudice stems from the white man's conscious or subconscious fears of the black man's allegedly superior virility. Indeed, quite a few of the sex jokes that men exchange are concerned with this subject, and any number of white males (who have never even seen a black man stripped) believe as an article of faith that the negro is equipped with an enormous phallus that makes him irresistible to women!

Of course, there are two 'phallic fallacies' here. Women aren't particularly interested in large penises and (as far as we can tell) there is *no* difference in size between the average black penis and the average white one. I can confirm this from my observations during two years of practice in a tropical country, when I must have examined several thousand black patients of both sexes. I could detect no structural differences between their genitalia and those of Europeans. Indeed, by far the largest male organ I saw during that time belonged to an Irish engineer; it may have been of significance that x-rays showed that he had abnormally dilated and tortuous blood vessels in the lower part of his body.

The Erect Penis

We've talked so far about the length of the male organ in its ordinary flaccid state. But how long should it be when it's erect? Well, the interesting thing here is that <u>most penises are very much the same size in erection.</u> The man whose non-erect organ is smallish will usually achieve about 100% increase in length during sexual excitement, while the man whose flaccid penis is on the largish size will probably only manage about 75% increase. In round figures, this means that the great majority of men measure between 15cm. (6″) and 18cm. (7″) in the erect position, with the average figure being about 16.5cm. (6½″). (Measurements taken on the dorsal side of the penis, which is the side nearer to the stomach.)

So you can see that even if a man genuinely has got an organ that is small when he's in the flaccid state, he's also got a built in compensating factor that will probably bring him up to not far off the same size as the fellow he sees in the shower room who *appears* to be vastly 'better equipped' sexually. Few males realize this fact, because few males (apart from homosexuals and sex researchers) ever see another man in a state of erection.

I hope that if you've stayed with me so far you'll appreciate that most of the time-hallowed male beliefs about the importance of a large penis are sheer nonsense. But there's one final point that's of great importance and that virtually every man forgets: it doesn't matter a hoot how long or how short your penis is—because the vagina is so cunningly designed that it will accommodate itself to any length of penis.

You see, the vagina of a woman who hasn't had a child is only a mere 7.5cm. (3″) long when she's not sexually excited. The figures for women who have had babies are only slightly different. And even when she has been aroused, her vagina usually extends only to a length of about 10cm. (4″). So it's obvious that any man's penis will fill her vagina completely, unless, of course, he happens to be one of those very, very rare unfortunates with an erect penile length of less than 4″.

You're probably wondering how on earth a man with an average length 6½″ penis manages to insert his penis into a normal woman's vagina at all. Well, the answer is quite simple—the vagina has the most remarkable capacity for lengthening if something is introduced into it *gradually*. So the exceptional man whose penis is, say, 20.5cm. (8″) long can still make love to literally any woman, providing he excites her properly and introduces his organ very slowly. If he does this (and do remember that word *gradually*) her vagina will quite happily lengthen by 150% or even 200% to accommodate him. The subject of the vagina is fully dealt with in the next chapter, *How a Woman is Made*.

So it's a remarkable fact that it is possible for any woman in the world to 'fit' with any man in the world, whatever the length of his penis. It's just as well that this is so because every man is stuck with the penile size he is naturally endowed with. I receive a lot of anguished letters from males who want to know how to add an extra two inches to their length, and my answer to all of them is that you can't alter your size—but if you would only realize it, you don't need to.

Anatomy of the Penis[1]

The flaccid penis is a small, flabby, floppy organ and a visitor from another planet who looked at one would never dream that the reproduction of the human race depended on this insignificant-looking structure! Figure 1 shows the flaccid penis in the circumcized and uncircumcized states—we'll come on to the question of the foreskin and circumcision later in this chapter.

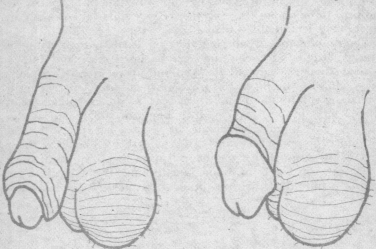

---

[1] *Widely known as the John Thomas, prick, cock etc.*

FIGURE 1

You can see that there's a small hole in the tip of the penis which looks like a very tiny mouth. This is the opening of the urinary passage, and it's also the orifice through which seminal fluid squirts at a man's moment of climax. (see Chapter Five: *What Happens at a Climax?*). The inside of the opening is usually rather hypersensitive and men don't like to be touched firmly here. Occasionally, people are stupid enough to poke things into it—this is dangerous and should never be attempted. (See Chapter Nine: *Is There Anything Wrong with Doing This, Doctor?*).

However, the smooth, rather plum-coloured area round the opening (the head of the penis, or *glans*) is richly equipped with nerve endings that convey highly pleasurable sensations up toward the brain, and stimulation of this area is immensely exciting for a male.

The glans varies a bit from man to man but is usually roughly

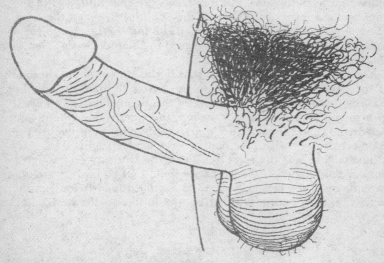

FIGURE 2

conical in shape. At the base of the cone, there is a ridge called the *corona*—you can see this in the drawing of an erect penis (figure 2). In childhood, the foreskin is attached to this ridge, and the two structures may not separate completely till adolescence or even early manhood. Sometimes a young man may be worried when he notices the last stages of this separation (thinking, naturally enough, that his penis is disintegrating), but there's actually no need for alarm. If the foreskin remained stuck to the ridge round the glans, it wouldn't be able to peel back properly in erection.

The shaft of the penis is covered in skin, through which large blue veins show. Many men have spent a lifetime afraid to ask anybody whether these are normal: they are! The penile skin is extremely sensitive (very nearly as sensitive as the glans, in fact), and stimulation of it by stroking, kissing and so on is immensely pleasurable for a man. The most satisfying areas vary from individual to individual, but most men prefer stimulation of the back and the front of the shaft of the penis, rather than the sides. (Techniques of penile stimulation, including the best ways for a woman to grip the organ, are discussed in Chapter Seven: *How to Handle a Man*).

You can see from the pictures that in the erect position the side of the penis that is further from the man's stomach is actually curved—many men are not aware of this unless they have looked in a mirror!—while the side nearer the tummy is straight and flattened. These are not just quirks of design—they enable the male organ to fit with precision into the female vagina.

The vagina and the erect penis are also tilted at very roughly the same angle (a fact for which we should all be fairly grateful). In some men, the penis comes up so far that it nearly touches the tummy, but in many others it rises only just to the horizontal.

Most people are about halfway between these two extremes.

The Foreskin and Circumcision

Every male is born with a foreskin or prepuce—the little sleeve of skin that protects the delicate tip of his penis during early life. I'm not going to go into the controversy on whether circumcision should be carried out routinely on all boy babies, except to say that personally I am against it, and that I'm glad to see that outside the USA (where circumcision is still regarded as an important social ritual) the operation is now being increasingly rarely performed.

A great deal of nonsense has been talked in the past about the effect, beneficial or otherwise that circumcision is said to have on sex. For example, the famous American psychiatrist Dr. David Reuben, in his book *Everything you Always Wanted to Know About Sex* claims that 'circumcision adds to sexual pleasure in many ways'. He's wrong.

Let's state categorically that whether you are circumcised or not should make no difference at all to your sexual function, unless your foreskin is too tight to slide back—or unless, of course, you are unfortunate enough to have been circumcized badly and have acquired a deformed penis as a result. Fortunately, this eventuality is rare.

In America, where circumcision is nearly universal, most men seem to have the idea that the uncircumcized male has an advantage over them. (Curiously enough, in England—where circumcision is now rare—one sometimes finds the exact reverse of this belief.) The story goes that the tip of the uncircumcized penis is less sensitive because the man still has his foreskin, and that this factor allows him to prolong intercourse for a longer period. In fact, Masters and Johnson showed in 1966 that there was no difference in sensitivity between the circumcized and the un-circumcized male penis. The only man who does need circumcision to help his sex life is the one whose prepuce doesn't retract (go back) fully when his penis is erect. Obviously if your foreskin is covering the head of your penis when you're making love, it's a rather unsatisfactory state of affairs; fortunately, this isn't common in men who have been taught to retract the foreskin since boyhood.

This leads us to a final word about the foreskin—the question of hygiene. Whether you're having sex regularly or not, you should of course pull it back and wash your penis properly with soap and water every day, to prevent the rather unpleasant cheesy material called 'smegma' accumulating. Not only is smegma very un-appetizing as far as love-making is concerned, but its continued presence can lead to inflammation and indeed (over a period of 50 years or so) to cancer. So from about the age of five (*not* before), little boys should be taught to retract the foreskin and wash them-selves. As long as this is done, there's usually no need whatever for circumcision.

The Testicles

The two male sex glands (widely known as the 'balls') which manufacture sperms by the billion, are called the testicles (or testes), and they hang side by side in the little bag called the scrotum.

As you can see from figure 3, each testicle is rather like a flattened golf ball in size and shape. Each one is about $1\frac{3}{4}''$ long, $1\frac{1}{4}''$ deep, and $1''$ thick.

But the actual size of these glands doesn't matter very much. Men who take great pride in the vast dimensions of their testicles are kidding themselves—a large one doesn't mean that a man is extremely virile or vice versa. Indeed, the commonest reason for apparently having an enormous testicle is the presence of a *hydrocele*, an abnormal accumulation of fluid which, while pretty harmless, usually needs tapping off, often with corresponding deflation of the ego of the erstwhile-proud owner!

It's quite common for one testicle to be slightly smaller than the other, and again this is nothing at all to worry about. If one of them seems to be very tiny, however, it's best to get it checked by a doctor—though even if it's not functioning, there's no cause for alarm. Fortunately, as long as the other testicle is normal, it will be perfectly capable of doing the work of two.

We don't really know why some testicles are very small. It used to be thought that in many cases this atrophy (wasting) was due to mumps. This is why in the past young men who have caught this disease have often been quite terrified in case the infection attacked the testicles and rendered them sterile or impotent. But

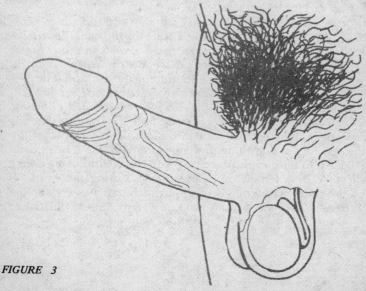

FIGURE 3

in fact we now know that the dangers of mumps have been greatly exaggerated, and though the virus very often does invade the testicles (producing a few days of quite unpleasant pain), it's very rare for any permanent damage to be done.

NUMBER AND POSITION. The great majority of men have two testicles though, once in a blue moon, one finds a patient with three. Contrary to folk mythology, this doesn't make him some kind of super-male; the extra gland is of no special value and usually it gets in the way so much that it has to be removed surgically.

A small number of people are born with only one testicle (or lose one in an accident) but they are usually perfectly normal men in every way, since once again the other gland can do the work of two. If a man feels very embarrassed about the lack of a testicle, a plastic surgeon would be willing to perform a simple cosmetic operation and insert a dummy one for him.

It's very common for people to *think* that a testicle is missing, when all that's happened is that it's stuck in the canal that leads down from the abdomen. The testicle should come down this canal before birth, and if it hasn't descended properly this ought to be spotted at the baby's first routine medical examination. A fairly minor operation will usually be required to bring it down.

If an adult finds that one of his testes is undescended he should see a doctor as soon as possible, because lasting harm (particularly to his fertility) may occur if something isn't done about it.

However, a man with undescended testicles isn't necessarily infertile. An English medical student with this condition once went to a lecture by a famous London surgeon, during the course of which the great man wrongly said that such patients were bound to be sterile. The young man promptly went outside and killed himself, but at his post mortem, the doctors found that he would in fact have been quite capable of fathering children.

In quite normal males it is fairly common for one or other of the glands to retire inside the mouth of the canal for a few minutes. It may get pushed up during intercourse, or as a result of a blow, or simply in reaction to some sudden external threat.

You see, all males are equipped with an interesting primitive reflex (called the cremasteric reflex) which whips the testicles up out of harm's way when danger threatens. If you wade into icy water, for instance, your sex glands will very sensibly draw themselves up as high as they can. A less traumatic method of demonstrating this reflex is to stand upright and to get some friendly person to jab the inside of your thigh a few times with the tip of a pencil. She will then be able to observe the testicle on that side (with a fine instinct for self-preservation) moving upwards in a series of hasty leaps and bounds! The testicles also move upwards during sexual excitement, and at the moment of ejaculation (coming) they are usually jammed right up against the body.

One final word on the position of the sex glands: many men are worried by the fact that one of their testicles hangs lower than the other. This is quite normal. In 85% of males, the left one is lower than the right one (and in most of the rest the right is lower than the left). Many intriguing reasons have been put forward for this strange phenomenon, but the truth is that we simply don't know why the male sex should have been designed in this oddly lopsided way.

The Scrotum (the 'pouch')
We've already mentioned the scrotum which is the bag of skin in which the testicles hang. It's a slightly odd looking structure, partly smooth and partly covered in deep wrinkles. It looks the

way it does because its main job is to be a radiator of heat.

You see, the testicles can only produce sperms efficiently if they're a few degrees below body temperature. (That's why an undescended testicle may well be malfunctioning.) So the two glands have to be suspended outside the body with only the scrotum to protect them. If the temperature of the testicles rises too high, the wrinkles of the scrotum immediately open out so that heat is lost. Correspondingly, if things are getting a bit chilly, the scrotum puckers up in order to conserve heat. Therefore there's no need to worry (as some people do) about the fact that after a dip in a cool swimming bath, your scrotum shrivels up to a rather pathetic-looking size—it's just doing its job of keeping your testicles at the right temperature. The relationship of the temperature of the scrotum to fertility is discussed in Chapter Thirteen: *Pregnancy and Sex.*

The scrotum is definitely one of the erotic areas of the body and most men like to have it stroked or tickled. A very odd practice has grown up in America in which the woman makes a nick in the man's scrotum and inflates it with a drinking straw. I only mention this in order to say how very stupid and dangerous it is. If you want to get an infected scrotum and possibly lose your testicles, this is the way to go about it.

How Does It All Work?

Well, we've considered all the parts of the male sexual organs that you need to know about. How does it all work?

It's really very simple. The testicle manufactures millions upon millions of sperms (up to about 500 million are produced in a single orgasm) and these travel up the tube which is called the *vas.* Male sterilization by cutting through the vas is called vasectomy—see Chapter Ten: *How to Prevent Babies.*

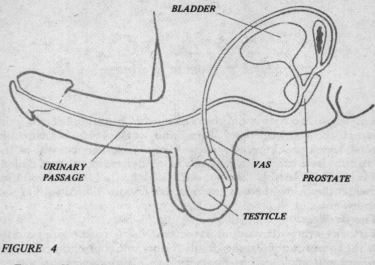

BLADDER

URINARY
PASSAGE

VAS

PROSTATE

TESTICLE

FIGURE 4

Eventually, the sperm enter the urinary passage just in front of the bladder. As you can see in the diagram (figure 4), this is the point at which the prostate gland adds its secretion to the seminal fluid; this secretion nourishes the sperms and keeps them active and lively so as to increase their chances of finding an egg to fertilize.

However, the prostate gland needn't really concern anybody under about 55. After that age, it very often increases in size and may create an obstruction to the flow of urine; this condition may necessitate a surgical operation. The subject is discussed further in the earlier book in this series, *The Home Doctor*.

The last part of the sperm's journey is down the urinary passage to the tip of the penis. Although this passage is also used for urination, it is in fact impossible for a man to pass water when he is in a state of erection, so the two fluids do not mix.

We'll look more closely at the way that sexual excitement leads to the squirting of seminal fluid from the penis (ejaculation) in Chapter Five: *What Happens at a Climax?* But first, let's move on to the very, very important topic of how a woman is made.

CHAPTER TWO
How a Woman is Made

The female body is a rare combination of beauty of design and superb technical efficiency. Men (and women) who want to be good lovers should get to know every nook and cranny of it, learning how each part responds to tender caressing and skilled love-making. In this chapter, we'll look first at the breasts and then at the below-the-belt reproductive organs (the vulva, vagina and womb).

The Breasts

Virtually every man would agree that the female bosom is one of the most beautiful things in all Nature. Of course, our attitude is very much coloured by the fact that we males (even the bottle-fed ones) have been obsessed by the breast since babyhood. (Why girl babies don't retain the same obsession is one of the great mysteries of psychology.)

Unfortunately this breast fixation has got a bit out of hand these days. Obviously, it does no particular harm that quite a lot of men cheerfully admit that when they meet a girl, they look at her bosom before they look at her face, but it is unfortunate that so many women obviously feel a deep sense of inadequacy about the size and shape of their breasts. Furthermore, though some men do actually *prefer* small bosoms, quite a few husbands are tempted to stray from the path of virtue simply because they rather foolishly feel that their wives don't match up to the enormous mammary dimensions of some film star or pin-up.

In fact, the pictures of glamorous girls that one sees are very often grossly misleading. A lot of these ladies are so plump that without their brassières and specially upholstered dresses they tend to collapse completely. Of course, there are quite a few youngish girls who photograph superbly well in the nude, because they genuinely do have the firm thrusting breasts (full of imaginary milk) that are so much admired today. But very often the naked pin-up's unbelievable bust-line has been achieved not by Nature but by artifice—perhaps the surgical insertion of silicone bags, and certainly with the skilful placing of lights and camera, the careful positioning of the body, the subtle use of breast make-up, and even the cunning application of Sellotape! Indeed, I understand that the centre fold pin-ups of a celebrated magazine have quite often been two or three months pregnant when photographed, a factor which gives them a distinctly unfair advantage.

What all this adds up to is that no woman should feel ashamed of the small size of her breasts, because the average bosom is very, very much smaller and less firm that most people imagine. In the picture (figure 5), you can see four different types of breast. Most women these days would probably wish to have as large a bosom as the girl on the right, but in fact it is the one on the *left* who is fairly average, at least among younger women.

FIGURE 5

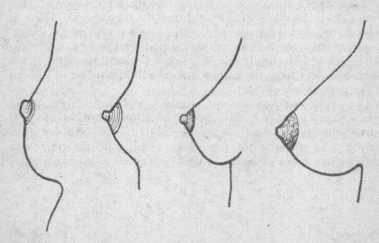

Sadly, there is very little you can do to increase the size of the breasts. Tablets and creams are useless and possibly dangerous. Water massagers may produce a slight temporary increase in size, but no more than would be achieved by the centuries-old technique of splashing icy water (or snow!) on the bosom. The most famous 'breast developer' in the world is simply a small exercising device, intended to add bulk to the chest muscles—not to the bosom itself. Really intensive daily massage by yourself or your partner over a period of months may cause at least some enlargement. (It may also lead to milk production — indeed, this technique is used by women who want to breast feed their adopted babies.)

The Pill *will* very often produce a moderate increase in size (rather like the swelling many women get before a period) but this advantage may sometimes be lost after a few months. Injections of liquid silicone has now been given up by most surgeons because it is too dangerous, but if you are really desperate you could get a plastic surgeon to insert a pair of silicone bags for you.

In general, however, I would agree with the celebrated Miss Diana Dors who quite frankly said that the only way she knew to produce significant enlargement of the bosom was to get pregnant. Unfortunately, the benefits of this method tend to be rather transient (lasting only until the baby is a few months old), and the technique does have the rather unfortunate side-effect of adding to the population.

The occasional woman who wants to reduce her breast size is in a happier position than the girl with small breasts. If she is overweight (as is almost always the case) she can do it by strict dieting. And if she is not, then she can ask a plastic surgeon to perform the breast reduction operation known as mammoplasty.

In any case it's very important for both men and women to realize that female sexuality and responsiveness have *no* connection whatever with breast size. There are many big breasted girls around who are completely frigid, and conversely there are a lot of flat-chested women who are extremely highly-sexed and superb lovers. It's true that the breast is a very erotic area of the body, but women who have a small bosom seem to get just as much pleasure from having their breasts stimulated as do women with large ones.

THE AREOLA AND THE NIPPLE. Techniques of breast stimulation are discussed in Chapter Six (*How to Handle a Woman*). In general, a lover's efforts should be chiefly directed toward the areola, (which is the pigmented ring round the nipple) and to the nipple itself (which is the raised part in the centre), mainly because these areas are richly supplied with sensory nerve endings.

You can see from the series of pictures in figure 5 that the normal areola may be of all sorts of shades and sizes. Very often, there are fine hairs round the edge of it. This is also quite normal, but if the hair is dark a woman may wish to have it removed for cosmetic reasons. Electrolysis by a skilled practitioner is the best method.

The nipple too varies quite a lot in shape and size, as you can see from the same picture. It tends to be darker and very much more prominent in a woman who has had children. Because it is the 'virgin' nipple outline that is most admired nowadays, mothers tend to be a bit sensitive about what many of them regard as the 'inferior' shape of their nipples, but this is quite irrational. Leaving the dictates of fashion on one side, a long, prominent nipple is just as inherently sexy as a shortish, cone-shaped one.

Incidentally, don't worry if your nipples are inverted (turned in). Many women are shaped like this and the only problem it causes is that it makes it a bit difficult to breast feed. If you want to alter the appearance, get hold of some maternity 'shells' from a chemist and wear them in your bra all day long; also, spend as much time as you can each day in drawing the nipples out with your fingers. Better still, have your mate do this for you, either with fingers or with lips.

Warning. If a nipple that has previously been normal becomes turned inwards, see your doctor as soon as you can. Similarly, go to him at once if you notice any lumps in the breasts. It is sensible for all women over about the age of 23 to check their breasts once a month (after their period) for these warning signs.

BREAST CHANGES DURING LOVE MAKING. When a girl is aroused sexually, the first thing that happens to her breasts is that her nipples stand out and become erect. Her bosom starts to get a little larger, and the blue veins on it may stand out more. The extent to which this happens depends mainly on the number of children she has breast-fed. Next, the pink or brown areola round the nipple becomes slightly swollen, and a warm coral or rose-coloured flush spreads over the whole bosom as the moment of climax approaches.

Once the orgasm is over, the 'sex flush' (as it is called) vanishes from the breast within a few seconds and the disc of the areola gets smaller again. Within about 10 minutes or so, the nipple itself starts to go down and the breast returns to its normal size—unless, of course, the woman is stimulated to another climax, in which case the whole cycle starts all over again.

These changes that take place in the breast are very similar to those that occur in the genital organs. For instance, erection of the nipples in sexual excitement is just like the erection that

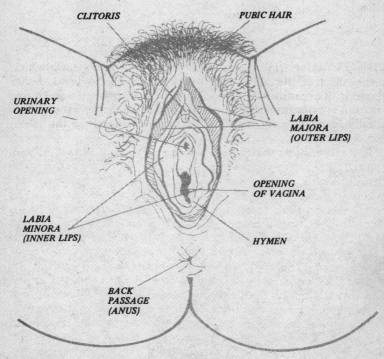

CLITORIS   **PUBIC HAIR**

URINARY OPENING

LABIA MAJORA (OUTER LIPS)

OPENING OF VAGINA

LABIA MINORA (INNER LIPS)

HYMEN

BACK PASSAGE (ANUS)

FIGURE 6

happens to a man's penis when he's aroused, and indeed, just like the erection of that all-important organ the clitoris, which we're going to discuss in a moment under the heading of The Vulva.

The Vulva[1]

This word (which puzzles many people) just means the *outside* of the female sex organs, the area you can actually see. The various parts of the vulva are shown in figure 6.

---

[1]*Because most people don't know enough about anatomy to distinguish the two, the vulva and vagina are both widely referred to as the pussy, quim, cunt, fanny, crumpet, etc.*

THE PUBIC HAIR. Let's begin with the pubic hair, which covers most of the vulva and which extends for several inches above it. This rather crisp and crinkly hair (which women are sometimes embarrassed about but which men find very exciting) usually forms a fairly neat and attractive triangle at the lower end of the tummy.

The exact shape varies from woman to woman, however, and

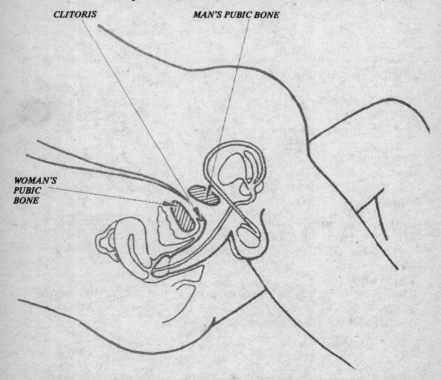

CLITORIS   MAN'S PUBIC BONE

WOMAN'S
PUBIC
BONE

FIGURE 7

while some girls sport a rather sparse growth reminiscent of a Van Dyke beard, others have thick and luxuriant pubic hair which spreads over quite an area. Both extremes are perfectly normal.

If the hair extends up the middle of the tummy towards the navel, or if it runs onto the thighs, it is usual to trim it back a little, but this is just a question of fashion—before the days of the bikini, this kind of tonsorial work was rare. Some girls (particularly those who are interested in naturism) do shave off all the pubic hair and this is quite harmless, provided, of course, that you are careful what you are doing with the razor. However, the vulva may be a little uncomfortable when the hairs regrow—as mothers who have been shaved for a delivery will know.

There is no truth in the belief that shaving the hair off is 'more hygienic'. Perhaps a more pertinent point is that some men do find it sexier to be able to see all the parts of the vulva which is why many strippers (and certain other ladies who exhibit their bodies for profit) remain shaved all their working lives.

Incidentally, virtually every woman's pubic hair is either black, brown, 'mousey' or red. Really blonde hair is very rare and the widespread idea that all natural blondes have platinum-coloured maidenhair is quite wrong.

THE PUBIC BONE. Like the pubic hair, the pubic bone is not strictly speaking part of the vulva, but it's convenient to mention it here. You can see it in figure 7 and you can feel its hard surface under the middle part of the triangle of hair. Its importance lies in the fact that during love play and intercourse it provides something firm against which the man can compress the woman's clitoris and surrounding tissues (we'll be coming to the clitoris in just a moment).

This is quite an important factor in successful love-making, because unless there were something to push against it would be rather difficult to stimulate the highly erotic upper part of the vulva adequately. In some quarters the act of love is inelegantly referred to as 'a grind'. However much one may deplore the terminology, the word does express very effectively the idea that during intercourse in the 'ordinary' (i.e. face to face) positions, the man's pubic bone very often does 'grind' against the woman's (as shown in figure 7), thus compressing the part of her body in which she feels the most delightful sensations of all—the clitoris.

THE CLITORIS.[1] Over the pubic bone and under the middle part of the triangle of maidenhair there is a soft pad of fatty tissue medically known as the *mons pubis* or *mons veneris*—a Latin expression meaning 'the mount of desire'. (A witty doctor once pointed out in the columns of an august medical journal that the term could be quite accurately translated as 'the fanny hill'.)

It is quite exciting for a woman to have this soft pad gently stimulated, but if you slide your finger-tips an inch or two down from here you'll find that you are over the clitoris itself.

You can see the clitoris in figure 6. Note its position clearly for, tiny as it is, it is more important, sexually speaking, than anything else in the female body (apart, of course, from the brain!)

I cannot stress too often for the benefit of male readers that it is the clitoris and its surrounding area to which a man should principally direct his attention when arousing a woman. (See Chapter Six: *How to Handle a Woman*.) Many (probably most) men still have the notion that a woman's highest pleasure comes from the vagina and this is *not* true.

In fact, vaginal stimulation with a penis, fingers or anything else is mainly effective *because of the extent to which it produces a 'tug'*

[1] *This is one of the few parts of the female genitals to have a 'popular' name; it is quite widely known as 'the clit'.*

on the exquisitely sensitive tissues around the clitoris. Only a few years ago, a great deal of nonsense used to be talked about the alleged differences between 'vaginal orgasm' and 'clitoral orgasm', and many doctors working in the field of sex relations held that a climax which originated in the clitoris was somehow 'immature'. With their typically male-orientated point of view (centred around the importance of hard, deep penile thrusting), they thought that a 'mature' woman only achieved satisfaction from an area deep within her vagina. Today we know that this is all wrong.

Now the reason why the clitoris is so sensitive and so all-important is quite simple—it is the exact equivalent of a man's penis. Indeed, in unfortunate people who are 'betwixt and between' the sexes, the problem is often to decide whether they have a large clitoris or a small penis.

If you examine the tissues of the clitoris under the microscope, it's quite obvious that they are very much the same as the tissues of the male organ. During sexual excitement, they fill with blood in a precisely similar way, so that the clitoris becomes erect and swollen. I should explain, however, that even an erect clitoris is *not* very big. A lot of women (having read that the organ is 'like a small penis') get a bit worried when they can't really find theirs at all! In fact, most of the body of the clitoris is buried under the skin and it is really only the head of the organ (which is usually no bigger than a very small button) that you can see.

I would seriously recommend any woman to take a small mirror and to lie down and hold it between her thighs. Identify the position of your clitoris carefully (observing that it is partly protected by a tiny 'hood' which is the equivalent of the male foreskin) and make a mental note that *this* is the place where your

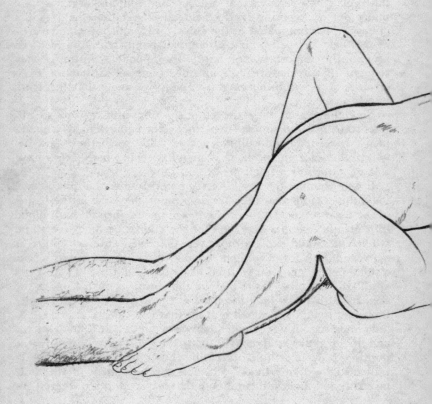

FIGURE 18

man should be gently stimulating you with his finger tips, his lips and his tongue. (See Chapter Six : *How to Handle a Woman.*)

There isn't, however, any particular need for him to stimulate your clitoris with his penis. This is another widespread misconception, and it grew up during the 1950s and 1960s when people began to cotton on to the idea of the great importance of the clitoris. Sex advisors (who should have known better) started telling men that it was desirable to ram the tip of the penis against the clitoral area during love play, and even during intercourse. This led to some mad pole-vaulting experiments, which were usually far from successful!

Of course it is quite nice if the glans (head) of the male organ bounces off the clitoris during its entry into the vagina, but it is hard to achieve more than this and it's really pretty pointless to keep pulling the penis out at each stroke and stabbing it in the general direction of the clitoris.

In practice, as we've said above, there's no problem : the thrust of a penis inside the vagina tugs on the lips of the vulva and so stimulates the clitoris very effectively. Furthermore, we've seen that in the face-to-face positions the man's pubic bone tends to grind against the woman's, thus giving *direct* stimulation to the clitoris, which is sandwiched between the two bony surfaces. In all other intercourse positions, it's a good idea if the man reaches round from time to time and gives his partner additional excitement by *delicate* rubbing of her clitoris with the soft pads of his fingers.

In the past few years, vast numbers of 'clitoral stimulators' have been sold in Europe and America (see figure 35 in Chapter 9). Most of these are rubber rings that fit round the base of the man's penis, though some come in sheath form. A projection on the upper side is supposed to rub against the woman's clitoris during inter-course and so add to her excitement.

In practice, I am rather doubtful about these devices. Quite a lot of women seem to be turned off by them, regarding them as much too mechanical for romantic love-making. Others find them painful or merely uncomfortable. It has been suggested that the stimulators are a help to women who are frigid. This could possibly be so, but up till now I have not come across a couple whose sexual problems have been alleviated by one of these rings or sheaths.

On the other hand, clitoral stimulators are quite harmless and the couple who buy one just for amusement's sake and who treat it as a frivolous aid to good fun sex may find that its occasional use lends a little extra humour and pleasure to their love-making.

The clitoris can also be stimulated by battery-powered vibrators (see Chapter Nine: *Is There Anything Wrong with Doing This Doctor?*) A considerable number of women do find this kind of gentle repetitive stimulation pleasant and relaxing, but in general it is nowhere near as effective as the skilled probing of gentle and loving fingers.

One final point—it doesn't matter how big or small your clitoris is (just as it doesn't matter how large a man's penis is). There is no correlation between size of this organ and sensuality or responsiveness. Even if you can scarcely find it at all, you have just as much potential for a happy and satisfying sex life as anyone else.

THE LABIA, OR LIPS. The vulva is very like a mouth which is one reason why the mouth is, psychologically speaking, such a tremendously erotic area. It has not one but two sets of lips, which keep it closed off from the outside world, protecting the front passage from germs and keeping it watertight. In sexual excitement the two sets of lips part widely to reveal the opening of the vagina, as in figure 6.

Lovers should know each other's bodies, and it's a good idea for a man to find time to settle down to examine (and admire!) the way his loved one is made. Similarly, as I've said earlier, it's well worth any woman's while to use a small mirror to inspect her own vulva, and see what is revealed when its lips are rolled back.

You'll note that the two outer lips (the *labia majora*) are quite plump, often darkly pigmented, and always covered with crisp maidenhair on the outside. It's very common, incidentally, for one lip to be longer than the other and I've known girls get into a terrible state of unnecessary worry about this. (The same is true of the inner lips, which we'll discuss in a moment.)

The outer lips are quite erotic areas (though nowhere near as sensitive to excitement as the clitoris), and women do like to have them gently stroked. Peel them back as shown in figure 6, and you'll see the whole of the two inner lips, (the *labia minora*), whose tips often project between the outer lips.

The inner lips are very much thinner than the outer ones, and are little more than folds of delicate skin which run upwards to meet in the region of the clitoris. Like everything else inside the female passage, these inner lips are a pleasant deep pink or coral shade. (The internal colour of the female genitals is, incidentally, the same in all races, regardless of skin colour.) During sexual arousal, the inner lips swell with excitement, thus providing a sort of extra little 'collar' round the base of the penis. They change colour too, taking on a scarlet or even wine-red shade that fades just after the climax.

THE URINARY OPENING. Now part the inner lips and you'll see that in the pink tissues about two inches or so below the clitoris is the little urinary opening (the urethra) which leads up to the bladder.

Inexperienced men occasionally try to push the penis, or the tip of the finger, against this opening; this is often painful and the agonized woman may well respond by 'tightening up' so that further love-making is difficult or impossible.

So in general, it's best to keep away from the urinary opening. Of course, it's inevitable that the man's organ will rub against it during intercourse, but he shouldn't ever deliberately poke it with his fingers or tongue.

Quite apart from the fact that the tissues of the urinary passage are easily hurt, it's very, *very* easy to introduce germs into it. In a woman, the passage is so short that these germs have only a short distance to climb into the bladder where they'll very likely produce a painful attack of cystitis. (This subject is discussed further in Chapter Twelve : *Trouble Down Below*).

In fact, 'honeymoon cystitis' is very difficult to avoid, but you can at least cut down on such infections by not poking around the urinary opening. Some people are foolish enough to put things into it (usually during masturbation rather than during love-making), and though this undoubtedly does produce a pleasant sensation for some women, it really is a very stupid thing to do. Not only does it introduce infection, but the objects used are frequently lost, with embarrassing consequences.

(Indeed, the pathology museum at my own teaching hospital boasts a long row of glass jars, containing objects of this type which had to be surgically removed from various unfortunate women's bladders—everything from hairpins and needles to pens

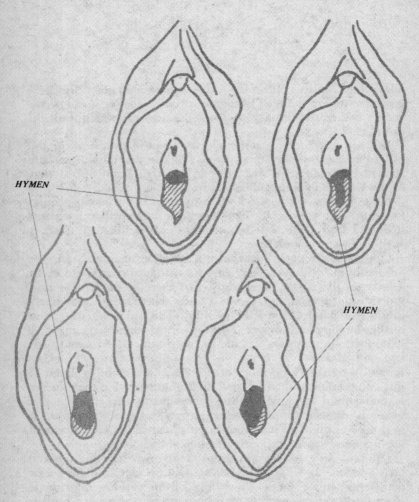

HYMEN

HYMEN

FIGURE 8

and pencils. At the end of the row is a jar containing three small fish. On seeing them, generations of astonished students have hastily looked up the museum catalogue, only to find that these specimens were *not* recovered from the interior of some over-sexed lady, but in fact caught by a former Professor of Pathology off Brighton Pier.)

The Hymen

When you peel back the inner lips (see figure 6) you'll see that below the urinary opening is a much larger hole, big enough to accommodate the shaft of the penis. This, of course, is the entry to the vagina, or front passage.

In a virgin, this entry is often partly closed off by the thin membrane called the *hymen*, virgin's veil, or maidenhead. It's hardly ever completely shut off (as people often think) for the simple reason that there has to be a gap for the menstrual blood loss to get through at each period. In those *very* rare cases where a girl at the age of puberty has a hymen without a gap in it, blood will dam up behind it and she will have recurrent monthly pains without any period. A simple operation will put things right.

The hymen may be all sorts of shapes (as shown in figure 8) but most commonly it's a sort of half moon across the lower half of the vaginal opening. It usually (though not invariably) gets swept away during the first act of intercourse, leaving only a few pink tags to show that it was ever there. Contrary to widespread belief, the process of breaking it should be pretty painless and accompanied by very little blood loss (sometimes none at all).

Of course, people are always blaming the virgin's veil for their failure to achieve sexual success. A bride may say that it's so tough, or so tender, that her husband can't penetrate her. She tells him to take things gently, and they may well go on taking things gently for the next 20 years, in a welter of mutual frustration. Every obstetrician is familiar with the embarrassed woman who turns up pregnant and still, technically speaking, a virgin. Indeed, a British newspaper once ran a 'religious' feature appealing for women who had had experience of virgin birth. The great majority of those who replied were under the impression that they had had virgin pregnancies because their hymens were still intact!

In practice, although a very small number of women do have rather thick hymens, the real trouble in most cases is usually that the wife isn't relaxing and that the husband isn't stimulating her properly. There's no lubrication, so the vagina remains dry, taut and tense; it's this, and *not* the hymen, that prevents the penis from entering, and what the couple really need is some skilled advice from a doctor.

A gynecologist can, of course, cut through the hymen (a procedure known as hymenectomy), but it's an encouraging sign of the times that this largely unnecessary procedure, once common, is now rarely performed outside the USA. American surgeons still do it quite frequently, sometimes as part of a 'premarital program' that involves internal examinations for both bride and groom, but in Britain and most other countries the majority of doctors take the view that there's one structure and one only that's intended to break through a healthy young woman's hymen—and it certainly isn't a scalpel.

Of course, the virgin's veil is a highly symbolic part of the female anatomy, and a great deal of fuss used to be made about it in the days gone by. Foolish old men used to pay unbelievable prices to sleep with young women who allegedly had intact hymens, and these ladies used to shriek convincingly night after night as they were deflowered for the ninety-third time! Until quite recently, many bridegrooms (especially in Catholic countries) made quite an issue of their brides' virginity; for instance, woe betide any Italian girl who did not have a few drops of blood on her sheets the morning after her wedding night. Indeed, a flourishing industry in replacing vanished hymens grew up among Italian surgeons!

But these days it is rare to find a woman over the age of 20 with much of a hymen. Not only, of course, do far more girls nowadays have premarital intercourse, but many hymens are broken by petting, by masturbation, or by the insertion of sanitary tampons, though it is quite possible to insert a tampon without breaking the virgin's veil as long as there is a fairly wide opening through it into the vagina.

It's common for women's magazines to say that maidenheads can be broken by the sort of energetic sports that teenage girls go in for these days. One approaches this statement with a certain cynicism, but in any case it is virtually impossible to prove or disprove.

However, the girl who is not a virgin and who is contemplating matrimony with one of the rapidly diminishing band of males who still insist on a wife coming to the marriage bed 'intact' need have no worries at all, for the fact is that hardly any men, no matter how experienced, are capable of distinguishing a virgin from a non-virgin. Contrary to what most people believe, even a doctor usually cannot tell whether a hymen is present simply by doing a routine vaginal examination. Only by using a special instrument to look inside can an experienced physician be reasonably sure what state the hymen is in (and even then there may be

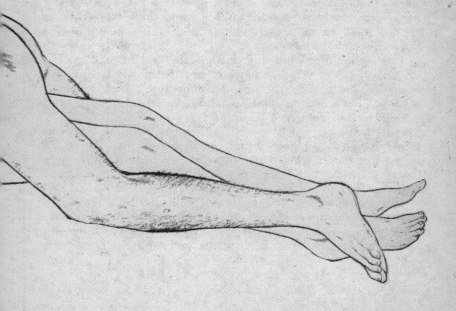

FIGURE 19

doubt). So ladies, unless you are marrying a virginity-obsessed gynecologist who proposes to bring a speculum and a torch on honeymoon with him, you can rest assured that your secret is safe—if you want it to be.

The Vagina

The vagina (the front passage), as wits have frequently remarked, is the original tunnel of love. It has one function in life and one only, and that is to accommodate the male penis, which it does admirably. You can see how good the 'fit' is by looking at figure 7. Indeed, if you've read the previous chapter (*How A Man Is Made*) you'll know that this quite remarkably well designed tube is capable of fitting snugly round virtually any male organ in the world, provided the owner of the vagina is wooed romantically and given a chance to relax! Women who think their vaginas are too small are nearly always suffering from vaginismus—see the next section of this chapter.

This is because, while the unstimulated vagina is about 3″ long, the walls of this love passage have the most extraordinary capacity for distension (they *must* have, because otherwise they'd never be able to accommodate something the size of a baby's head during the last minutes of labour.)

Indeed, the vaginal cavity is much larger than most women think, though rather smaller than many men imagine. There are a vast number of women who have the notion that their love passages are tiny little crevices, liable to burst at the seams if any man were to put his penis inside.

This is quite wrong, and doctors who work in this field usually advise these patients to explore the cavity for themselves. Typically, what happens is that a woman who has been terrified all her life of putting anything into her vagina, and who has even been afraid to use sanitary tampons, is quite astonished when she finally plucks up courage to put her finger inside. Here within her is this splendid, roomy passage, extending upwards and backwards for several inches, with soft, well-upholstered comfortable walls and a pleasant dewy secretion that lubricates the opening and makes it easy to slip in and out. The subject of normal and abnormal vaginal secretion—i.e. discharge—is dealt with in Chapter Twelve : *Trouble Down Below*.

Until quite recently, doctors used to believe that this love juice, which not only makes intercourse possible, but which helps to make it so delightful, came from the neck of the womb and from certain specialized glands around the vulva. Thanks (once again!) to Masters and Johnson, we now know that this is not true. In fact, it is the vaginal walls themselves that pour forth the secretion. By actually inserting a camera into the vagina, the distinguished American sex researchers were able to show that if a man starts to arouse a woman sexually, the first thing that happens is that the walls of her vagina begin to secrete droplets of the love fluid in considerable quantities. This remarkable mechanism ensures that within a matter of 30 seconds, the woman is moist enough to allow entry of the man's penis.

No sensible husband would normally come in as early as this however, because there are, of course, *two* factors which decide whether entry is comfortable—lubrication and muscular relaxation. Let's look now at the muscles which have to relax in order to make love-making happy and successful.

THE VAGINAL MUSCLES. Around what sex researchers slightly inelegantly term 'the barrel' of the vagina are quite powerful 'love muscles'. Most of the time, these muscles keep the vagina closed off fairly tightly, like a mouth saying 'No.' Indeed, in many an unhappy woman, the muscles clamp down hard whenever a sexual approach is made to her—a condition called *vaginismus*. This disorder is dealt with fully in Chapter Eleven: *Problems with Sex*, but it's worth pointing out that a mild degree of vaginismus occurs in very many inexperienced women and that in fact, it is extremely hard for any girl (particularly one who has never borne a child) to relax her vaginal muscles and open up her love passage just at will.

Happily, the techniques of love play (see Chapter Six: *How to Handle a Woman*), applied in a romantic and loving atmosphere will make the vaginal muscles relax and open up so that, instead of saying 'No', they give an emphatic 'Yes' to the penis that wants to enter! This process of relaxation may take anything from two to thirty minutes, however, so the golden rule for a man who wants to be a good lover is—don't rush things.

Once the penis is in, the vaginal muscles do to some extent automatically close down around it, which is nice for both partners. Swelling of the vaginal walls brought on by sexual excitement also contributes to this 'gripping' of the penis.

But the 'grip' is not all that tight, particularly in a woman who is already a mother. The more children you have, the more lax your vaginal muscles are likely to become, especially if the babies are big or the deliveries are difficult.

So it's a good idea for women to practise exercising the love muscles to try to keep them in tone so that they will contract snugly around the penis during intercourse. These days, some obstetric hospitals are very good about encouraging women to exercise the muscles after delivery, but others don't seem to bother very much, which is a pity, especially as lax pelvic musculature leads to prolapse as well as diminished enjoyment of sex for both partners.

I'd recommend therefore that any woman who has had a child should try to exercise these muscles for about 20 minutes every morning and evening. This is no problem, because you can do it while you're at work, or cleaning the house, or cooking, or washing or, indeed, even making love.

All you do is to contract the pelvic muscles hard and repeatedly just as though you were trying to hold back the flow of urine or a bowel action. Six months of doing this every day will tone your vagina up remarkably.

American gynecologists, who lead the world in this field, have invented a device called a perineometer which gives a reading of the contractile strength of the love muscles. If a mother's reading is below a certain level, she is given an exercise programme, and if it's really low she'll probably be advised to have a repair operation.

Girls who haven't had babies needn't worry about keeping their love muscles in trim, but it's a nice idea if they make an effort to contract the muscles during intercourse. If this is done properly, the man can feel it, and it's very pleasant for him.

Some writers have claimed that perfect control of the love muscles enables a woman to perform the most extraordinary feats of massage on a man's penis, in effect 'milking' it from base to tip. I rather take leave to doubt this notion, but anything's possible, I suppose, and it is not beyond the bounds of credibility that some sultry siren could achieve such fantastic muscular control that she could do this. Certainly, a respected doctor quite recently claimed that a foolish and flirtatious ballet dancer had attempted much the same thing on his examining fingers, making it impossible for him to withdraw them until he had given her

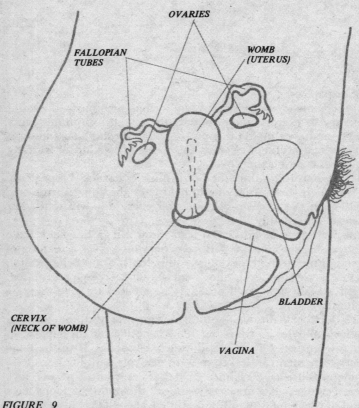

OVARIES

FALLOPIAN
TUBES

WOMB
(UTERUS)

BLADDER

CERVIX
(NECK OF WOMB)

VAGINA

FIGURE 9

a very stern lecture on the stupidity of her action!

However, let me close this section by saying that I simply do not believe there is the slightest truth in the many stories which circulate in men's clubs concerning ladies whose vaginal muscles are allegedly capable of clamping down on a man's penis so hard that he cannot withdraw it. If anyone thinks he can prove me wrong, I shall be interested to hear it, but frankly I regard this as one of those myths which simply demonstrate the accuracy of Freud's theories about male castration fears!

A similar but rather nastier myth widely believed among credulous men is that women of certain races have teeth inside the vagina. Here the castration symbolism is very obvious indeed.

The Womb and The Ovaries

I shall say very little about the womb, because there is only one part of it which is of any significance in love-making. You can see from figure 9 that the neck of the womb (the cervix) projects down into the vagina, where it can be felt as a smooth knob, rather like the tip of somebody's nose.

Any woman who uses a cap during intercourse *must* be able to identify her cervix (for the reasons why, see Chapter Ten: *How to Prevent Babies.*)

A man who wants to be a really good lover should find out where it is too, by slipping both his index and middle fingers into the vagina and reaching up to the top. Many girls do not seem to have any sensation at all in the neck of the womb, but others definitely do, and these women will often enjoy having the cervix gently prodded or even grasped and moved around. It's worth trying the experiment.

You can see where the ovaries are located in figure 9. Very advanced lovers may be able to produce agreeable sensations in their wives by stimulating the ovaries with gentle movements of the fingers against the vaginal walls, but there are few men who have either the skill or the anatomical knowledge to do this, and it is not generally recommended.

The function of the ovaries (together with that of the womb) is discussed in the next very important chapter: *How Sex Leads To Babies*.

CHAPTER THREE
How Sex Leads to Babies

Practically every new novel I have read since about 1960 contains a seemingly obligatory scene in which the hero makes intoxicating love to the heroine (or sometimes to the villainess). I suppose this is all very well and it's certainly a refreshing change from the sort of books that were usually written during the previous 150 years or so, with their generally sexless characters and complete absence of realisation of physical love.

But one thing worries me about modern novels. There's hardly ever any reference at all to the simple fact that sex leads to babies. None of those entrancing girls whom James Bond or his successors make love to ever gets pregnant (though admittedly unwanted pregnancies do occur in a few less 'glamorous' novels.)

Indeed, when do we ever read of a hero pausing in the midst of the excitement to enquire whether the lady he is about to have intercourse with is protected against conception? When do we read of a dashing young man having the sense to stop and reach into his pocket for a packet of condoms? Never, presumably because writers feel it would spoil the romantic atmosphere!

Though I've been talking about this rather light-heartedly, the fact is that these modern books, and also modern films which portray 'careless love' as the ideal, do lead people to forget the simplest and most basic fact of life—that intercourse causes babies. No wonder that unplanned and disastrous pregnancies occur!

So this short chapter will describe the relationship between sex and conception, while the actual techniques of contraception will be discussed in Chapter Ten: *How to Prevent Babies*.

The Sperms

The sperms are formed in the man's testicles and come shooting out of his penis in his seminal fluid when he reaches his climax (see Chapter Five: *What Happens at a Climax?*) But be warned—

those few dewdrops of clearish fluid that men often produce long before their climax may well contain sperms—which is one reason why the 'withdrawal method' of birth control is so unreliable (and also why a sheath has to be put on *before* intercourse starts and *not* halfway through).

Inside the Vagina

When the man reaches his climax, the teaspoonful or so of fluid he produces is deposited in a pool at the top of the woman's vagina. As you can see from figure 10 her cervix (the neck of her womb) is normally just above this teeming pool of sperms and in fact, as she relaxes after her orgasm, her cervix will gently dip into the fluid so that the sperms can swim up into the interior of the womb.

FIGURE 10

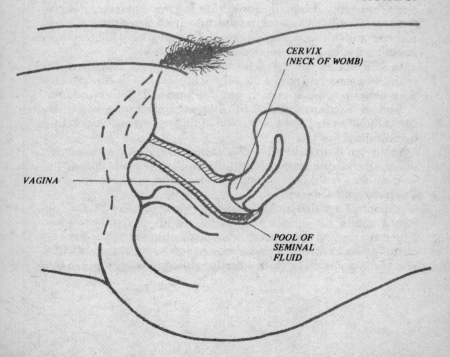

Female Orgasm and Conception

It's important to realize that the girl *doesn't* have to reach a climax for pregnancy to occur. Many women have this idea, and those who are both 'frigid' *and* having trouble in conceiving often blame themselves because they think it is their inability to reach orgasm that is preventing conception. In fact, if you think about it, there have been countless women who have been unfortunate enough to conceive after being raped, so it's quite obvious that no female emotional response at all is necessary for pregnancy to occur.

But does it help conception if the woman reaches a climax? For years many doctors believed that this was the case, thinking that the womb sucked sperms up into itself at orgasm. In fact Masters and Johnson's researches have shown that there simply doesn't seem to be any suction effect.

Indeed, for rather complex reasons it appears that there are many women who stand a slightly better chance of conceiving if they become sexually excited but don't actually reach a climax. A woman who has already had children, for instance, will retain the pool of seminal fluid at the top of her vagina for longer if she doesn't quite 'come'.

I must stress that any effect that the female climax has in cutting down the chance of pregnancy is probably *very* slight. Most women need not concern themselves with this problem.

Position and Conception

The pool of seminal fluid forms just where the cervix will dip into it only if the woman is lying flat on her back, as shown in figure 10. So, for the average woman this position gives the best chance of conception. The woman who has a retroverted womb— one which points backwards—needs a different position if she is to stand the best chance of .pregnancy. See Chapter Thirteen: *Pregnancy and Sex.*

However, so much seminal fluid gets splashed around the vagina when the man reaches his climax that most women can really get pregnant in virtually any position. There's a question that flows in endlessly to those of us who run advice columns, asking if it is true that it's impossible to get pregnant if the couple make love standing up. The answer is that although standing does increase the speed with which the seminal pool runs out, this will make virtually no difference, except to a subfertile couple. Yet because of the extraordinary persistence of the standing-up myth, many babies continue to be conceived in this uncomfortable and inconvenient position!

What Happens in the Womb and Tubes?

You can see the womb and the tubes in figure 9. One egg (ovum) comes out of one or other of the ovaries each month (a process called ovulation) and makes its way down the tube and into the womb. If no sperm arrives to fertilize it, it'll be lost in the blood flow at the next menstrual period.

If sperms *are* around at the right time however, there's every chance that fertilization will take place. Just a single one of the hundreds of millions of tiny sperms released during a male climax, or before at any time during intercourse, can fertilize an egg and thereby start a pregnancy.

Once this happens, the fertilized egg will embed itself in the wall of the womb. The first warning the woman will have that this has happened is when she misses a period.

When is the Right Time for Conception?

This is an important fact that every sexually-active woman should know—but which very few of them seem to be aware of! Ovulation

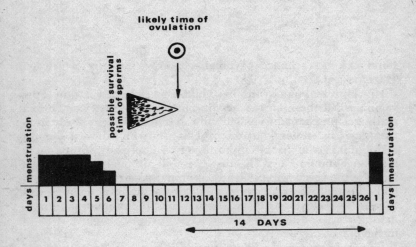

FIGURE 11

(egg-release) normally occurs about 14 days before the start of a period. So, a woman with a 28 day cycle is probably most likely to conceive 14 days after the start of her last period, while someone with a 26 day cycle is most liable to become pregnant about 12 days after the beginning of menstruation. You can see this in figure 11.

However, one cannot say *for certain* that ovulation will take place at this time. There are many women whose ovulation day simply cannot be predicted in this simple way, though they may be able to work it out by temperature chart method. See Chapter Ten.

This is one reason why the 'rhythm method' of family planning at present favoured by the Catholic Church (the 'safe period') is unfortunately somewhat unreliable. Although most girls do conceive in the middle of the month and are *relatively* safe if they confine sex to the time around the period, accidents will happen with this method quite frequently.

How Long Can Sperms Survive?
Once inside the woman's body, they can probably survive for 24 to 48 hours. In some instances they can be alive and wriggling for very much longer. This is the other reason why the 'safe period' method is unreliable. Look at figure 11 again and you'll see that a woman whose ovulation takes place on day 12 of her menstrual cycle could quite possibly get pregnant by having sex, say, eight days after the start of a period.

Can You Conceive by Just Having Sex Once?
Yes. Some people have the idea that you must have intercourse a number of times before conception will take place and that 'once doesn't matter' or that 'five minutes can't do any harm'.

In fact, many women actually do conceive the very first time they have sex, often after only a few seconds of intercourse, though this would be rather bad luck (or good luck, depending on your point of view).

It's very hard to be certain, but it seems likely that the chances against an unwanted pregnancy in a single unprotected act of intercourse are about 25-1 or 30-1. These may seem quite long odds, but the risk just isn't worth taking when really good contraception measures are available for pretty well everyone.

In my own view, anyone who embarks on a sexual relationship (inside or outside of marriage) should always make absolutely sure that pregnancy cannot occur—unless the couple are deliberately trying to have a child. At this late stage in the 20th century we shouldn't be having countless abortions and illegitimate and unwanted babies, because there's really no need for most of these mistakes to happen.

In other words, *if you're having sex, you should be using contraception.* You'll find the reliable methods detailed in Chapter Ten: *How to Prevent Babies.*

CHAPTER FOUR
How to Make Love

Of course, no-one can really tell you how to make love in just one short chapter. But since up till now we've been looking at the anatomy and physiology of love in a factual and clinical way, let's try and put it all together and see how a really expert couple would make love under ideal romantic circumstances. I hasten to add that there's obviously no need for a novice lover to slavishly follow every move we describe!

Let's imagine then that the man and the woman have been out for the evening, have enjoyed each other's company and are now returning home in a loving and tender mood. Though they have known each other a long time, the man doesn't neglect to whisper endearments in the woman's ear and she responds with warm affection, nuzzling her head against him, stroking his thigh, and exciting him with flirtatious hints about the fun they are going to have later on.

So when they reach home, both of them are in a pleasantly elevated state of sexual tension. He takes her in his arms and covers her lips, her neck, and her breasts with kisses. Before long, he is gently helping her out of her clothes, while her caressing hands move lovingly over his body.

Soon they are both naked. But (as an old hand at the game) he doesn't make the mistake of immediately rushing straight into intercourse. Instead he caresses her body gently and deftly, letting his fingers and his lips roam over every nook and cranny. He knows exactly where to stroke, where to press firmly, where to kiss and where to nibble with exciting little love-bites.

The woman too is skilled in the ways of love. She uses her lips and body to arouse her man to an ever-higher pitch of desire, squeezing him, hugging him, kissing him, caressing his penis, and urging him on with sweet murmurings of love.

Naturally, she herself becomes immensely excited during all this. Her heart pounds, she breathes more quickly, and even her skin will become warm and pink with desire. If skilfully caressed, she may reach one or more climaxes before she is ready to be penetrated.

By this time, the man's control is almost at breaking point, but when she urges him to enter her he is experienced enough to be able to subdue any urge to reach an immediate orgasm. Instead, he gently slips his penis into her and begins with long, slow thrusts to excite her even more.

Five, 10, 15 minutes pass and the couple are still making love, sometimes wildly and furiously, sometimes slowly and tenderly, sometimes pausing to exchange erotic compliments or indulge a mutually exciting fantasy, and sometimes switching to a different position so as to give each other new and delightful sensations.

But eventually both partners sense that the time has come for the entertainment to reach its finale. The girl may by now have had quite a few climaxes, but she gathers her strength for one last special effort. The man quickens his pace, thrusting ever more deeply inside her as the rhythm speeds up, building up to the final superb moment of mutual orgasm.

So it's all over. But perhaps not quite over, for the two lovers still lie with limbs entwined, enjoying the pleasant feeling of satisfaction and mutual tenderness that is called the afterglow of love. Before long they fall asleep in each other's arms, warm, secure and happy at the close of a memorable evening.

If love-making is always like that for *you*, then you probably have no need of this or any other book. Otherwise, read on . . . .

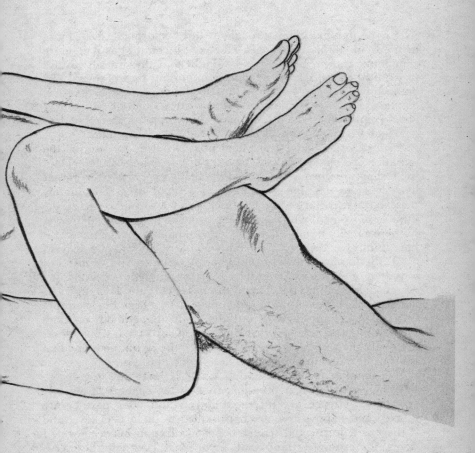

FIGURE 20

CHAPTER FIVE
What Happens at a Climax?

As I hope to make clear throughout this book there's a lot more to sex than simply reaching a climax, or 'coming' as it is more commonly known, but there's no doubt that the orgasm (to use its medical name) is a tremendously important part of sexual life. Somebody who can't achieve this explosive release of pent-up emotion usually feels immensély frustrated, though he or she may not recognise the fact. Many neurotic symptoms are related to orgasmic frustration, particularly in middle-aged women.

A lot of writers have tried (and usually failed) to describe the sensation of a climax. In fact, it's very nearly impossible to explain the feeling to someone who's never actually experienced it, rather like trying to describe a rainbow to a blind man. Fortunately these days there are very few men (and a steadily decreasing number of women) who haven't enjoyed this delightful experience, so there's really no need for me to try to paint word-pictures of it here. But if you *can't* reach a climax do please see Chapter Eleven.

All I'll do now is to point out that in both men and women the sensation of an orgasm does vary a lot on different occasions. It's no good expecting the Earth to move (to use Hemingway's famous phrase) every time you make love—because it simply won't. Some climaxes are very trivial affairs that embody no more pleasure than, say, that of drinking a good cup of tea, while others are really shattering experiences in which the fortunate individual (or pair of individuals) virtually loses consciousness.

You simply can't forecast what kind of climax you're going to have on any particular occasion, though the chances of a really ecstatic experience are increased if you and your partner are relaxed and happy, if you're both skilled in the arts of love, and if there is a warm and tender bond of affection between you. I don't, for example, think that anyone has ever felt the Earth move in a five minute encounter with a prostitute.

The Male Climax

What happens when a man reaches his orgasm? There's no need for us to go into all the scientific technicalities here, except to say that when a man has been making love for a variable period of time (anything from 30 seconds to 30 minutes or longer, depending on his control) there comes a moment when he knows that a climax is inevitable. A skilled lover can easily take himself up to the brink of this moment and then calm down again, only going 'over the top' when he and his partner are ready.

The moment of going 'over the top' is the moment when seminal fluid floods into the lower end of the pipe (the urethra) that runs up through the penis. The fluid distends this pipe very rapidly, blowing it out to two or three times its normal width. This not only produces an immensely pleasant sensation in the base of the penis, but provokes a tremendous series of contractions in the muscular wall of the pipe. It is these powerful muscle contractions that drive the fluid out of the penis in a series of about half a dozen surges, strong enough to send the white pearly drops spurting anything up to 12 inches away.

How much fluid should there be? The average is about two to six ml. (a teaspoonful is 5ml.). A lot of men think that they produce much, much more than a teaspoonful, but this is often just a bit of male vanity!

The volume varies a lot, however, and it is likely to be temporarily reduced (sometimes to almost nothing) by repeated climaxes. The stores of fluid may take a few days to build up to normal again, which is why a couple who are deliberately trying to have a baby should build up a 'reserve' by abstaining from sex for a few days before concentrating all their efforts on the time

FIGURE 12

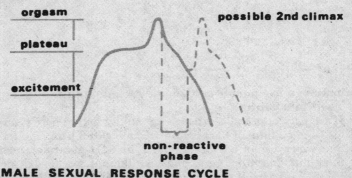

MALE SEXUAL RESPONSE CYCLE

around ovulation. (See Chapter Thirteen: *Pregnancy and Sex*).

There are anything from 60 million to 100 million tiny sperms in each ml. of seminal fluid, which means that the tiny amount produced at each climax could, in theory, father some 500 million human beings, or about one sixth of the population of the world. Happily, nature has so arranged it that this does not happen!

How soon should a man be able to reach another climax? This is a very difficult question, because individual males vary so much. Furthermore, a man's capacity for repeated orgasm tends to diminish markedly over the years, which is why one sometimes meets a man of 25 who is deeply worried about his potency because he can only make love four times a night instead of five.

The writer and journalist Frank Harris, who died about half a century ago, expressed this very neatly. He said that as a boy his father had given him a target rifle; later he had been entrusted with a double-barrelled shotgun, and as a grown man he had fired a machine gun. But, he pointed out, 'my *Heavenly* father did things the other way round.' As a teenager, his sexual capacity had been that of an erratic and wildly uncontrollable machine-gun; it was only in later years that he had acquired what he called a precision single-shot rifle!

Harris had some odd ideas about sexual physiology, but he was right in this matter. As Dr Alfred Kinsey showed in his famous

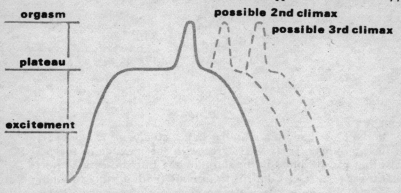

FEMALE SEXUAL RESPONSE CYCLE

report *Sexual Behaviour in the Human Male*, 1948, about 20% of 15-year old males can reach a repeated climax but less than 10% of 25-year olds (and less than 5% of 40 year olds) do the same thing.

However, the mature man reaps the benefit of being able to control his orgasm far more efficiently, and this is one reason why a male is likely to be a much better lover at 40 than he was at 17, even though his capacity for climaxes in a single evening may have dropped from perhaps six to one.

In fact, he probably *could* do more than this if he and, more particularly, his wife really set their minds to it. You see, the reaction of a climax (which is shown graphically in figure 12), has been somewhat inelegantly compared to the flushing of a cistern: after it happens, there's a non-reactive phase during which there won't be any response no matter how hard (or how repeatedly) you try! Then, before full recovery, there's a period during which a really powerful stimulus will produce a reaction. So, many 'one shot men' (to use the American expression) could reach a second climax 30 minutes or so after the first if their wives really set about rubbing their penises with vigour and enthusiasm. But it's worth pointing out that quite a lot of people have a sensation of extreme tenderness in the penis after a climax, and these men literally cannot bear to be touched there for anything up to an hour.

On the other hand if a man has to get up and go to work early in the morning he may well agree with the message of the post card that can be found in the shops of any English seaside resort: beneath a picture of a knight in armour (with a sadly drooping lance) are the words 'Once a king, always a king—once a knight is quite enough!'

Are too many climaxes bad for a man? No, not at all. It's a common myth that too much sex 'is bad for the health', 'weakens the blood', or 'weakens the back', but this is all nonsense. When your body has had enough it won't respond any more, and that's that; so it really is impossible to have too many orgasms. Obviously, repeated love making can cause tiredness next day, but apart from that the only possible side-effects are soreness and, occasionally, a transient swelling (oedema or edema) of the penis —which can be alarming but which always passes off in 24 hours or so.

So men who worry about whether having four or five climaxes a week will harm their health can relax. Indeed, Dr. Alfred Kinsey was able to find six men—a lawyer, a labourer, two doctors, a scientist and a schoolteacher—who had each averaged more than 10 orgasms a week for over 30 years, and one of these (the lawyer) had achieved the rather staggering figure of 33.1 weekly climaxes over this long period without any damage to his health—a remarkable testament to the stamina and dedication of the legal profession.

How many climaxes a week does the average man reach? In case any readers feel a trifle inadequate in the face of these rather astonishing statistics, I hasten to add that according to Kinsey the average male reaches only about $2\frac{1}{2}$ climaxes per week (if you see what I mean). There is considerable individual variation, however, with younger men naturally tending to achieve higher frequencies. About 8% of the adult male population are in the habit of making love (or reaching orgasm by some other means such as masturbation) every single night of the week, and conversely, about 15% of all men have one climax (or less) every fortnight.

So the range of normality is very wide. It's important to bear this in mind and not to make the common mistake of assuming that our own behaviour is the absolute norm to which all other men should aspire.

Let's close this section with a story to illustrate this point. During the Second World War (in the 'dark ages' before Kinsey published his statistics), an American judge granted a woman a divorce on the grounds of her husband's 'insatiable sexual appetite'. Indeed, when he heard how often this depraved character wanted to make love, the scandalized judge promptly had him committed to a mental institution. You may be surprised to learn that the evidence which so horrified the court was that the husband liked to have intercourse as often as *three times a week*. Thanks to Dr. Kinsey and his researches, that particular kind of judicial folly is never likely to happen again.

The Female Climax

What happens when a woman reaches her orgasm? Here again, I don't propose to get too technical. Basically, what takes place in physical terms is that at the moment of orgasm, most of the muscles of the woman's body go into a kind of involuntary spasm (which is why her face becomes contorted into a grimace almost like that of pain). The tissues around the mouth of her vagina (which have become swollen with excitement so as to form a sort of 'collar' round the base of the penis) contract in a series of powerful and immensely pleasurable waves that come at just about the same interval as the 'surges' that accompany the man's climax. Muscular contractions also take place in the womb, but whether the woman can actually feel them is doubtful.

Incidentally, these changes *don't* help conception to occur (see Chapter Three: *How Sex leads to Babies*), so there's no need for a woman to hold back to keep herself from getting pregnant.

In a purely physical sense, that's about all that happens at a woman's climax. There's an extraordinary persistent myth to the effect that girls, like men, produce a gush of fluid at orgasm (see for example John Cleland's famous novel, *Fanny Hill* written over 200 years ago and still going strong), but this is complete nonsense.

Should every woman be able to reach a climax? In theory, yes— if her sexuality has not been maimed by a repressive childhood in which she was given the idea that intercourse was dirty, painful or frightening. Seventy or 80 years ago, few people had even *heard* of a female climax, and those who did know of it mostly believed that it could only be achieved by 'loose women' and prostitutes. As late as the 1950s, many medical students were being told that 25% of women were 'constitutionally frigid', a doctrine which is now known (happily) to be not in accordance with the facts. It seems probable that in the present day only about 5% to 10% of sexually active women are finding it impossible to reach a climax, and the number is steadily decreasing as society becomes progressively less inhibited.

However, it's important to stress that while men can reach orgasm pretty well as soon as they get to puberty (and often before) this isn't at present true of most women, though this fact may be due simply to the degree of repressive conditioning that society still imposes on the female. According to Kinsey's figures, only just over half of all women have experienced a climax by the age of 20.[1] Of married women aged 16 to 20, some 20% had not yet reached orgasm, which seems to confirm the generally held view that many normal women do require several weeks or months of sexual experience (through intercourse, petting or masturbation) before they reach their first climax.

Should a woman reach a climax every single time she makes love? Ideally, yes—but it doesn't particularly matter if she doesn't, as long as she herself isn't frustrated. Plenty of women enjoy the warm, tender sensation of lovemaking and the thrill of exciting their partners, without very much caring whether they themselves achieve an orgasm on each occasion.

Unfortunately, there's a bit of a tendency to sexual athleticism these days, by which I mean that people regard themselves as 'failures' if they don't 'perform' superbly well every time they make love. It's a good thing that women (and men) want to make themselves better lovers, but it's obviously foolish to be so obsessed by performance that you become tense and anxious in bed.

So, if you do really feel frustrated by not reaching a climax every time, read the advice in Chapter Eleven: *Problems with Sex,* and, of course, get your husband to look at Chapter Six: *How to Handle a Woman.* But if you're happy as you are, don't let Mrs Jones down the road with her tales of 14 orgasms a night make you feel inadequate. In your own way, you're probably just as good a lover as she is.

What's the truth about multiple climaxes? You can see from figure 12 that women are far better equipped than men to reach more than one orgasm. Oddly enough, until about 25 years ago, people scarcely ever heard this phenomenon mentioned. A very

---

[1]Sexual Behavior in the Human Female, *published in* 1953. *This was, of course, well before the advent of the 'Permissive Society', and it is virtually certain that a lot more young women of* 20 *would have experienced a climax today.*

good popular handbook of sex which was very widely read in the 1950s said that repeated climaxes *might* perhaps be possible among passionate, hot-blooded Mediterranean women but were *most* unlikely in the case of cool, restrained British or American ladies! This, of course, was in the era when people of North European descent firmly believed in all those sadly-unfounded myths about the great skill and sexual capacity of 'Latin lovers', both male and female.

In 1953, Dr. Kinsey shattered quite a few complacent illusions by showing that about 14% of women do have multiple climaxes. But most of them averaged only about two or three orgasms each time they made love, and the ability to reach more than four climaxes was rare. The most 'passionate' group of women were those aged 41 to 45, but only 2% of these ladies were in the habit

FIGURE 21

of enjoying more than four orgasms at a session of love-making.

I would say that in the less inhibited society we live in today, multiple female orgasm is probably a lot more common than it was. There are certainly some women around who regularly reach six or ten orgasms in a night, and a really sensuous girl with a skilled husband can sometimes achieve as many as 20 major or minor climaxes at one session, though she will probably feel absolutely exhausted (and not a little sore) next morning.

But let me stress again that performance for performance's sake in bed is absolutely pointless. The wife who reaches a single climax pretty well every time she makes love is doing well, and certainly has nothing to worry about.

Mutual Orgasm

Finally, just a word about this business of reaching a climax at the same moment, 'coming together'. For many years sex manuals made a big thing about this, urging on couples the necessity of reaching the 'supreme moment' at precisely the same split second. The result was inevitable. Thousands of people developed all kinds of anxieties about the fact that they found it rather difficult to 'come together'.

And, of course, the truth is that while really skilled lovers can do this every time, in the early days of love-making it's very unlikely that two inexperienced human bodies will manage to synchronize with each other to this extent. But the point is that it *doesn't matter*. Love-making can be perfectly satisfactory if one partner reaches a climax two, five or even 10 minutes before the other one, just as long as neither of them has the idea that they have 'failed' by not having a simultaneous orgasm.

In such cases, it's commoner for the man to 'come' first.[1] Obviously he should try to restrain this tendency but (particularly

---

[1] *Any man who invariably comes after only a very short time is suffering from premature ejaculation and needs help—See Chapter Eleven:* Problems with Sex.

if he's young) there's no need for him to worry about it for he'll get better control as time goes by. In the meantime, what he must do, of course, is to make sure that (having had a few seconds to recover after his orgasm) he brings his wife to *her* climax by finger or tongue stimulation (see Chapter Six: *How to Handle a Woman*).

Unfortunately, what happens in many cases is that the husband simply goes to sleep after reaching orgasm, leaving his poor frustrated wife to lie awake in a state of unresolved tension for the next couple of hours or so. This is unforgiveable—and totally unnecessary.

There is much less of a problem (indeed, no problem at all) if the woman reaches her climax first, for all she has to do then is to lie back and enjoy the sensation of her man coming inside her (and, indeed, consider the possibility of reaching a second orgasm herself!)

So mutual climax definitely *isn't* essential. It's very nice when it happens—but love-making can be just as nice when it doesn't happen!

CHAPTER SIX
How to Handle a Woman

Sex is wonderful, but good sex isn't easy. A lot of people talk as though it were the simplest thing in the world. They seem to imagine that two healthy young people, without the least amount of training or teaching, should be able to achieve a perfect relationship right away. This impression is fostered by romantic books and films in which boy meets girl, they gaze into each other's eyes, and—bang!—a flawless mating takes place, with both of them seeing celestial fireworks at the same time.

Unfortunately, life isn't like that. What happens far, far more often at a first love-making is that the man fails to excite the woman properly, she tightens up, he can't get in and therefore pushes harder, she squeals with pain, and he (in a flurry of anxiety and frustration) reaches his climax far too early. *Not* exactly the stuff that dreams are made of. It's no wonder that so many wedding nights turn into a fiasco.

Now the answer to all this is simply *love play*. When couples come to me and tell me about their mutual lack of success in bed I usually ask them how long they spend caressing each other before the man attempts to enter. They very often reply either that no love play takes place at all, or that it's confined to a few minutes.

Now although there should be no fixed rules, timetables, or stopwatches in bed, my advice to these couples is always to spend *a full half hour* in exciting and arousing each other before actual intercourse begins. Even with much more experienced lovers it's a good idea to devote a little while to preliminary love play nearly every time. Although many women do *occasionally* like being taken rather roughly and abruptly, most girls, most of the time, do prefer gentle, gradual arousal through skilled love play techniques.

Love play is nice for men as well, and in the next chapter (*How to Handle a Man*), we'll be looking at ways in which a wife can provide fun and excitement for her husband.

But now let's examine the techniques whereby the male can please the female. Remember—he doesn't do this just for amusement's sake. He does it with the object of bringing her body to a high pitch of excitement so that certain remarkable changes will take place in it.

He wants to make the muscles round her vaginal opening relax, so that instead of being tightly closed they will slacken and open up to admit his penis. He wants to make her vaginal secretions flow so that her love passage will be moist, well-lubricated and welcoming. He wants to make her heart pound with excitement, so that it sends the blood racing round the sensual parts of her body—her genitals, her breasts, her lips, her tongue. He wants to make every part of her ready to receive him, and to arouse every nerve-ending to such a height of frenzy that she will eventually beg him to penetrate her and satisfy her.

Well, you can see that the average chap isn't going to learn to do all that overnight! In fact, I would say that it usually takes a willing, keen young man a matter of two or three *years* to become a reasonably skilful lover, and that's assuming that he reads as much as he can about the subject, that he's making love regularly with a partner who is uninhibited, resourceful, inventive, and (in plain words) fun to be with in bed.

It's very hackneyed to say that a woman's body is like a fine violin. But there's an awful lot of truth in the remark, and if you want to be good at love play, you should take a few tips from the concert violinist: *prepare yourself properly beforehand*; *learn your techniques*; and *practise, practise, practise!* And of course, it's helpful —though not essential—if you have a responsive instrument to practise on in the first place!

Preparing Yourself for Love Play

I saw a woman recently whose problem was a very common one. 'Before we were married, my husband was so neatly turned out. When he came to see me he looked lovely—all clean and nice and smelling of after-shave. No wonder he used to sweep me off my feet!'

Indeed, their love-making *before* marriage had been highly successful. Nowadays, things were very different.

'He comes to bed all unshaven and smelling of beer and doesn't even bother to clean his teeth or take his vest off. Then he wonders why he can't get me worked up!'

A bit of advice on personal hygiene to this lady's husband helped their problem considerably. For it's a basic rule that no woman is likely to respond to love play unless the man who is caressing her has paid her the compliment of making himself reasonably attractive.

One can't expect a paunchy 45 year old husband to look like love's young dream, but one can expect him to arrive in bed in a fairly presentable state. Two thousand years ago, the Roman poet Ovid wrote a splendid book called *The Art of Love*, in which he explained that before love play even began the male should make sure he is properly groomed and, in particular, that he smells nice and has trimmed his finger nails. (This is *very* important. Many a wedding night has been ruined because the groom caught a jagged nail on the bride's most delicate tissues and caused her intense pain and heavy bleeding.)

This advice of Ovid's was thoroughly sensible, and just as true today as ever it was. When the book was published, Ovid was promptly banished from Rome—an interesting comment on the changelessness of human stupidity where sexual matters are concerned! The man who invests in a bottle of after-shave lotion and some pleasantly scented talc has a head start where love play is concerned.

The Techniques of Love Play

VERBAL TECHNIQUES. There are a few (a *very* few) women who can actually be roused to a climax by having 'sweet nothings' whispered in their ears. Seldom is a girl *quite* that passionate, but virtually all women place a great deal of value on being verbally complimented in bed. Telling them how beautiful, how adorable, and how sexy they are forms a very important part of love play.

It's my impression that men are a great deal better at this sort of thing these days. Twenty years ago the average Anglo-Saxon male thought it was rather undignified to say romantic things to a woman—that sort of stuff was strictly for Latin lovers! Indeed, a lot of middle-aged couples still make love in a kind of embarrassed silence, as if they were terrified to say anything to each other. In the more inhibited days before the permissive society, it was claimed that at the end of intercourse some English wives would break the long silence by enquiring solicitously: 'Feeling *better*, Charles?'

So, don't forget to say romantic things. Don't forget too to say 'I love you' (assuming, of course, that you mean it) because those three words are probably more erotic than anything else on earth.

There's also a valuable place for a more robust form of verbal love play. Many couples quite uninhibitedly use basic four letter words to urge each other on in bed, and there's nothing in the

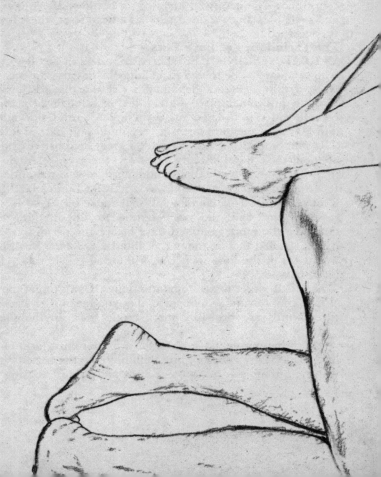

FIGURE 22

least wrong with this. Indeed, it can be a most valuable technique.

However, it's fairly obvious that a man should employ considerable caution when he first tries this out. A smart sophisticated career girl who uses the odd expletive herself now and then will probably enjoy it, but a wife who has been primly brought up may be more than a little shattered!

Quite a lot of men still think that women relish very coarse and obscene jokes in bed, but this is rarely so. Many a girl has been turned off by her mate trying to tell her verse 34 of some bawdy clubhouse ditty just when she's feeling all cosy and romantic!

So, if you want to use basic language to arouse your mate, be careful how you do it. The best way is to treat the whole thing as a bit of a joke remembering that many, but not all, women enjoy the sheer humour of using and hearing words that in other contexts they would consider 'rude'.

There is of course one great advantage in employing Anglo-Saxon terms as a form of verbal love play for at least your mate will understand what you're talking about! Few people, even in these so-called enlightened days, know the proper names for the various parts of their sex organs, but most of them do at least know the 'non-proper' ones. Your wife may not understand the word 'vulva' (though I hope she will after reading this book!), but she'll have heard one of the Anglo-Saxon equivalents.

Even if you both happen to be professors of anatomy, you may find a phrase like 'What a lovely little vulva' not only sounds a trifle artificial, but has considerably less erotic effect than 'What a beautiful little pussy' (or whatever synonym you prefer).[1]

CARESSING THE WHOLE BODY. Love play should begin with kisses, and with caresses. But it's important for the man to

---

[1]*An account of such terms is included in Chapter One:* How a Man is Made *and Chapter Two:* How a Woman is Made.

caress the woman's whole body—*not* just the sexual parts. The rule that the female usually likes to be aroused *gradually* applies with special force here. So start a good long way from the vagina and work *slowly* toward it. One night you might begin by gently stroking your partner's ankles, calves, and knees, before moving on to her tummy and thighs. Another night you could start with her neck and arms before slowly working downwards, and so on. Only very occasionally should you try the variation of immediately directing your attention to the vaginal area.

You will find after a while that you become quite expert at teasing and titillating, at stroking your loved one's thighs and belly while just occasionally letting your finger tips brush tantalizingly past her pubic hair. This kind of thing is far more exciting for a woman than a direct 'frontal assault'!

CARESSING THE EROGENOUS ZONES. After kissing and stroking the woman's body for a little while, you'll find it effective to shift your attention to what are called the 'secondary erogenous zones'. This is a bit of a mouthful of a title, but all it means is the areas of the body which though they don't form part of the sex organs are themselves sexually responsive. Erogenous zones vary a little from woman to woman, but almost always include the mouth, the breasts and the buttocks. We'll come on to these three major areas in a moment, but don't forget to direct your attention to the various nooks and crannies of the body, which are usually fairly sensual places. So too are the back of the neck, the lowest part of the spine, the palms of the hands, and the area behind the knees. Caressing and kissing all these places should have highly desirable results.

But go easy in your explorations. Some women are ticklish or dislike being touched in certain parts of their bodies. Others find it annoying if you touch them over-gently, and much prefer firm stroking to a light, delicate caress. You'll have to find out for yourself what suits your mate best, and be guided by her responses.

Wherever your hands go, your mouth should go too— not just kissing gently, but nuzzling, licking and nibbling, softly blowing, and of course, murmuring endearments.

HER MOUTH, HER BREASTS AND HER BUTTOCKS. These are the three most important secondary erogenous zones.

FIGURE 23

The mouth, I need hardly say, is one of the most highly-charged sensual areas of the female body. Surprisingly, quite a few men are so busy doing other things in bed that they forget the importance of simply kissing their wives on the lips! Whatever other kinds of exotic activity you are getting up to, don't forget this simple but vital part of love play. Nor should you confine yourself just to pressing lips against lips—experiment with pushing your tongue deep into your wife's mouth (French kissing), with running the tip of your tongue round the inside of her lips and cheeks,

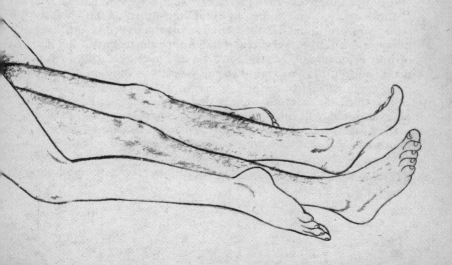

and with turning your head, right round so that the rough *top* surface of your tongue rubs excitingly over the top surface of hers.

As to *the breasts*, instinct tells most men what to do here. The most popular manoeuvre is simply to cup a breast in each hand and to squeeze gently and rhythmically. Stroking the area round the nipple turns many women on, but you should experiment for yourself to see what your partner likes best. Kissing and sucking the nipples is usually exciting for both male and female, but don't overdo it. The nipple is a delicate and sensitive part of the body and violent suction on it can *hurt!* Don't forget to try stimulating the very end of the nipple with the tip of your tongue—this can be very erotic.

You'll find that if you use these methods of breast caressing effectively, your mate's nipples will stand out firm and erect, and indeed her bosom will increase slightly in bulk (though only for a few minutes). You may possibly be able to bring her to orgasm by stimulating her breasts alone, though this is not likely —it is much more effective just as a technique of stimulation.

Incidentally, don't forget to compliment her on her breasts while you are doing all this. In this mammary conscious age, many women have very real (and quite unnecessary) feelings of inferiority about their bosoms. So any nice remark you can make will not only increase her enjoyment but may do wonders for her self confidence.

The third major erotic area is that of the *buttocks*. Practically all women enjoy having their bottoms caressed and squeezed and many of them like the sensation of being laid face down across a man's knees so that they are completely defenceless!

When squeezing the buttocks you can apply quite a lot of pressure since the tissues are far less delicate than those of the breasts. It's also quite safe to give little slaps and pinches, and it's useful to alternate these with long, gentle strokes. Take the opportunity to make occasional forays through her thighs so that your fingers briefly and tantalisingly touch the area near the vagina before returning to continue their stimulation of the bottom.

Quite a lot of people write to my advice columns enquiring whether it is alright to caress *between* the buttocks. There is nothing at all wrong with this, but you should bear in mind that there are likely to be more germs here than in most other parts of the body. Therefore a hand that has caressed this area should *not* afterwards be allowed to touch the vaginal region before washing carefully.

'LOVE BITES' AND 'LOVE SLAPS'. This is another subject that worries people. During love play (and, indeed, during intercourse itself) it's quite normal for both partners to give and receive tiny amounts of pain. This seems an illogical quirk of human nature, but it's a natural and practically universal trait. Since time began, all lovers have squeezed and hugged each other just up to the point where pain begins—and then stopped. However people who want to inflict or receive *severe* pain are in need of medical help. This subject is discussed further in Chapter Nine: *Is there Anything Wrong With Doing This, Doctor?*

So by all means excite your mate (and yourself!) with love bites. The favourite sites are the neck, the shoulders, the palms (especially the fleshy mound at the base of the thumb) and (most of all, to judge by the number of tiny bruises one sees on young women) the breasts.

But be careful how you apply your teeth to the bosom. These are pretty delicate tissues, so try to suck hard against the teeth

rather than giving a sharp bite. It's usually better not to apply love bites to the nipple itself, since if you misjudge things it can be pretty painful. Similarly, never give love bites around the vagina opening as the possibilities of doing damage are far too great.

Love slaps are usually delivered to the bottom, but (if done *gently*) they can be applied to other areas as well. A surprising number of women will actually reach a climax while their buttocks are being 'spanked' in this way. A young American student who pretended to be a doctor specializing in sexology persuaded a large number of college girls to help him with a 'research project' to investigate female reactions to bottom-smacking. He was able to pursue his 'studies' undisturbed for many months before one of the girls finally complained to the college authorities. Allegedly, she had been one of the large majority who had pronounced the sensation agreeable. But smacking should not be overdone. The dividing line between high enjoyment and real pain is a fairly narrow one, and it's rather easy for a heavy male hand to accidentally descend with more force than was intended.

CARESSING THE CLITORIS. By now let's assume that you've been cuddling and caressing for anything from five to 20 minutes. During that time, you'll have repeatedly brushed your fingers past the vaginal area, or perhaps momentarily pressed on it with your thigh. If you've done your job properly, your mate will now be more than eager for you to turn your attention directly to her most intimate parts. Indeed, she may well be clasping your hand and guiding it insistently to her vulva.

You should find that things are pretty moist there by now, since her vaginal secretions have had plenty of time to start lubricating the opening of the love passage. If she is still rather

FIGURE 13

dry, simply lick your fingers and use the moisture as a lubricant.

From figure 6 and figure 13, you'll see where the clitoris lies, and where to put your finger tips. You don't have to locate it exactly—just gently place the pads of your fingers on the approximate spot and rub upwards and downwards, an inch or two either way. Every now and then vary this by stimulating the whole area with the flat of your hand.

You can rub moderately firmly, squeezing the soft tissues against the pubic bone (which is the hard surface lying just under the triangle of pubic hair). However do bear in mind that the little clitoris itself (being very similar in structure to your own penis) is usually rather sensitive, so pressure should be *gently* applied and it is best to move away very briefly from it from time to time before returning with some slightly new technique of rubbing (for example, moving your finger-tips in a circular fashion). Keep 'scooping' up a little moisture from the vaginal opening just below and applying it to the area of the clitoris. If the vagina remains very dry despite all your efforts, you can buy a lubricant jelly—KY jelly—without prescription. Vaseline is an emergency substitute, but is rather greasy.

Learning to stimulate the clitoris properly takes time and you will not become expert at it within a matter of weeks, or even months. Early attempts at clitoral stimulation are usually pretty inept, so if you're in doubt about what to do, *don't* just blunder clumsily on—this is the time to ask your partner to show you how *she* likes it to be done.

If you use the technique properly, your mate will soon be very excited indeed. What you do next depends on your preference, and, more important, on hers. If she is capable of reaching more than one climax, then there's no reason why you shouldn't bring her to the first orgasm *now*.

Many passionate women like to have anything from one to ten climaxes through manual stimulation of the clitoris, before they ask their husbands to enter them.

Should your mate be a one-climax girl (and that's quite usual), then you may well want to take her near 'the brink' by rubbing her clitoris and then penetrating her. The best thing is simply to be guided by her demands—if she begs you to come in, then come in. If not, then there are lots more fascinating ways in which you can excite her.

USING THE FINGERS TO STIMULATE THE VAGINA. (*Warning*: there is no point in trying to master the very skilled caresses described in this section until you have become really good at stimulation of the clitoris). This is a very important technique (or rather, group of techniques) based on the fact that a man's middle finger fits quite neatly into the vagina.

Always use your right hand for this caress (assuming, of course, that you're right-handed), because to do it properly requires a great deal of coordination and skill. Clumsiness (which is inevitable among the inexperienced) very readily causes bruising or tearing of the delicate vaginal tissues, as well as temporary injury to the urinary passage (with resultant 'honeymoon cystitis'). Please, *please* make sure your nails are properly trimmed before you start!

With your palm *upwards*, gently slip your middle finger into the now-moist vagina. You may be able to feel the cervix (or neck of the womb) at the top end. You'll find that when the middle finger is right inside, the knuckles of your forefinger are resting on the area of the clitoris, as shown in figure 14. Begin moving your hand back and forwards, slowly at first and then more

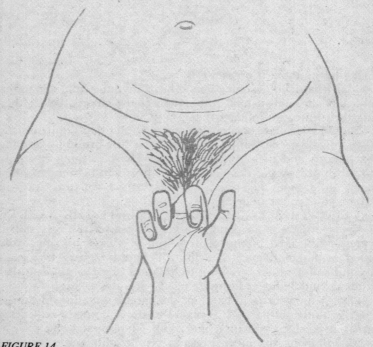

FIGURE 14

rapidly as you get the hang of it. Not only will the movement of the middle finger in the vagina produce delightful sensations for your partner, but the constant friction of your knuckles against her clitoris will give her the most exquisite excitement. (Note, however, that some women do not get very much pleasurable sensation from the inner part of the vagina; where this is the case, you will do better to concentrate on clitoris stimulation alone.)

As you grow more experienced, you can vary the rate and direction of your thrusts, trying (for instance) circular motions, deep long strokes, or very rapid short to-and-fro movements. In the early stages, *beware of drawing the finger too far out at each stroke—* this increases the chance of catching the delicate tissues with your nail.

In time, you can try such variations as putting in both the middle and the index finger, which should definitely enable you to feel the cervix—moving it around may be exciting for your partner, though women vary greatly in this respect. A very skilled lover can use the two-finger technique to feel his mate's ovaries, and some women enjoy having these stimulated. (This is, however, much too ambitious a form of love play for most people).

CUNNILINGUS (SOMETIMES SPELT CUNNILINC-TUS). This is one of the most delightful of all love play techniques. It simply means kissing your partner's vulva. Unlike the finger techniques, it is relatively easy to master in a fairly short time.

If you wish, you could begin at the moment in your love play when you've decided that it's time to move from stimulating the rest of the body to concentrate on the vaginal area. Simply bend downwards and apply a few kisses to the upper part of your mate's pubic hair. Gently move your lips an inch or two downwards until you are in the area of the clitoris (your partner's enthusiastic reaction should tell you that you're in the right spot). Then use your lips and tongue to bring her to a high pitch of excitement. Your tongue should slide back and forth over the clitoris in a regular movement, very much as you would do with your finger.

When you have learned to do this, try the effect of actually pushing your tongue into her vagina and moving it rapidly in and out. This is a highly effective method of stimulation that most women enjoy very much. For the inexperienced man, it takes a little getting used to, particularly because it is sometimes difficult for him to draw breath. The wife should therefore take care to keep her thighs well apart so that he can get some air!

This technique works best with one partner (it doesn't matter which) lying on top of the other (as shown in figure 15)—the wife

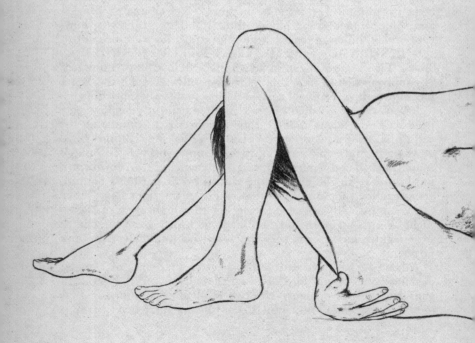

can then stimulate her husband's penis using one of the methods outlined in the next chapter, *How to Handle a Man*. Almost as convenient is for the couple to lie on their sides on the bed, with their heads between each other's thighs (the celebrated '69' position—so called because the two bodies are supposed to resemble the figures 6 and 9).

FIGURE 15

Alternatively, the wife can be flat on her back with her legs wide apart, while her husband lies on his front between her thighs, with his face against her vulva. All sorts of variations of cunnilingus can be worked out by an inventive couple—for example, many a woman enjoys standing naked on the floor and being stimulated by the tongue of a man kneeling at her feet. Or, if you like, your wife can sit in a chair (or on the edge of the bed) with her legs spread wide apart, while you bring her to orgasm with gentle, loving movements of your tongue.

Practise, Practise, Practise . . .

Remember what we said at the beginning of the chapter about the concert violinist's secrets of success. You won't become absolutely perfect at any of these love play techniques in a matter of a few days. So just keep trying, as often as you can. If one thing doesn't seem to work for you and your partner, leave it for a few nights and return to it later; in the meantime, try some of the other methods outlined in this chapter. And don't feel confined to the techniques of love play we've described here. If you can think of something else that gives your wife pleasure and excitement, go right ahead and do it—and *keep* doing it until you're really good at it!

Though you have to practise hard if you want to be a skilled lover, there's no need for you to take love play (or indeed sex itself) *too* seriously! Don't forget that the phrase 'love play' means what it says—it's part *love* and part *play*. Although it's a wonderful way of expressing your love for a woman, it's also meant to be sheer good, honest *fun* for both of you.

So, go ahead and enjoy yourselves. Laugh your way through love play, for laughter and spontaneity in bed are precious gifts, more valuable than ten thousand orgasms.

CHAPTER SEVEN
How to Handle a Man

Love play isn't just something that men do to women. Love play is a *mutual* thing—a splendid way of showing affection, tenderness and good honest desire for each other. A woman should play her full part in all this—for the days are gone when girls were expected simply to lie back and let their menfolk have their wicked way with them!

Unfortunately there are still quite a lot of wives who don't take an active enough role in love play. This is a great pity because all too often the result is that the husbands turn elsewhere for consolation. A man who left his charming, beautiful and intelligent wife to run off with a rather dowdy-looking girl from the office said: 'The difference between them is that Karen behaves as if she loves me when we're in bed while my wife lay flat on her back for 20 years and never lifted a finger to try to give me any pleasure.'

It's a common misconception that to be 'good in bed', a woman has to have enormous breasts and some sort of supercharged vagina. This is absolute nonsense. By and large, the seductive sirens of history (and of the present day) have been distinguished mainly for their personalities and for their skill in love play. Many of them have been fairly plain girls with flat chests and no particularly outstanding sexual capacity, yet they have known what to do to please a man. The wise wife would do well to follow their example just as the sensible husband ought to learn how to give pleasure to his wife. See Chapter Six: *How to Handle a Woman.*

What is a woman trying to do in the course of love play? Simply to arouse her mate, to make him hungry with desire for her, and to let him have all the excitement that is in her power to give. Of course, if he's functioning well sexually, he doesn't actually need love play in the physical way that she does. (As the previous chapter explained, it's very difficult for a woman to have intercourse with comfort unless she has been skilfully aroused.) But it does provide him with that extra incentive to spur him on— 'it's the icing on the wedding cake,' as one contented husband put it.

However, there are times when a man's flagging virility does need something to stimulate it, and in these circumstances love play is a physical necessity, rather than just the provider of grace notes to the melody of love. Again and again I have seen men who have become partly or completely impotent, or whose desire is waning with the passing years.[1] Very often all that is required is for the wife to roll up her sleeves and simply get down to work on her husband's penis. The effect of tender ministrations of skilled fingers can be almost magical in such cases. Unfortunately in some cases the wife is so shocked by the whole idea that she simply will not do it, or else the husband is too shy to ask her. If they had learned the techniques of love play together when they were young, there would very likely be no problem, but at any age new techniques can be mastered and can become a natural part of love-play.

If you've read the previous chapter, *How to Handle a Woman*, you'll know that I've suggested that it's a good idea for couples to spend quite a time on love play (perhaps even up to half an hour or so) before intercourse. This gives you, the woman, plenty of time to go through those physiological changes that are essential for successful love making. The main alterations that take place in your body during this time are a gentle relaxation of the mouth of your vagina (your vulva) and a great increase in the lubricating flow of your love juices.

[1] *Impotence and other male sexual problems are dealt with in Chapter Eleven:*

Now, no such preparatory changes take place in your mate. Once he's got his erection (which is normally almost instantaneous as soon as he starts thinking about making love to you), he's potentially within about 30 seconds of reaching a climax. So the most important rule for you to remember during love play is this: *don't over-stimulate him*, or he'll come before either of you are ready.

This is one of the common disasters of what are aptly termed the thrills and spills of wedding nights. The eager young bride, head full of techniques acquired from a marriage manual, attacks her groom's penis with gusto. He (poor chap) is already at a high pitch of excitement and anxiety; before he can stop himself, the whole thing's over in one unexpected ejaculation.[1]

If your husband is capable of repeated climaxes, it doesn't matter if your love play does make him reach orgasm very early on in the proceedings, but many males (including most of those who are past the first flush of youth) are what are inelegantly but succintly termed 'one-shot men' which means that once they have had an orgasm, that's the end of love making for the next couple of hours or so.

The remedy is quite simple. Always pay attention to the little signals your man gives as you stimulate him—his breathing, the noises of pleasure he makes in his throat, and the expression of excitement on his face. You'll soon learn how to tell when he's coming up to a climax, and that's the time for hands (or lips) off. Similarly, when he says 'Stop!' make sure you do so at once. Most men like to be taken to the very brink of orgasm during love play, and one extra stroke by you may take him over that brink, with disastrous results as far as that evening's entertainment is concerned.

---

[1] *Where over-eagerness—called premature ejaculation or 'hairtrigger trouble'—is a serious and continuing problem, medical advice is needed. See Chapter Eleven.*

Preparing Yourself for Love Play

Before we get down to the basics of what you're going to do to your mate, there is just the little matter of preparing yourself. It should go without saying that no man wants to spend half an hour romping on a bed with a frowzy creature dressed in bedsocks and wearing curlers! Unfortunately too many women (particularly those who've been married 10, 20 or 30 years) completely forget this point—or, perhaps it would be more accurate to say, refuse to recognize it.

This may seem a trivial thing, yet my impression is that the sexual side of many marriages breaks down because the wife simply won't pay her husband the compliment of beautifying herself at bedtime. Characteristically, the man says that *before* they got married the girl he took in his arms was always nicely made up with an attractive hairstyle; if they went to bed with each other she made sure that she was wearing the kind of exotic lingerie that turned him on, but nowadays, it's cold cream all over her face instead of false eyelashes, and a woolly vest instead of

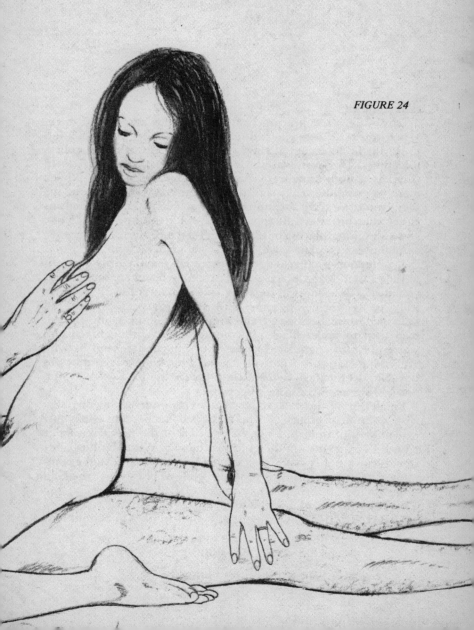

FIGURE 24

slinky undies.

Obviously, there are practical problems for any woman here. When you're a housewife and mother (or a career girl with a job to do in the morning) it's awkward not to go to bed in rollers sometimes. However you *should* be able to let your hair down (literally as well as figuratively) most nights of the week. What's more you can also make sure that whenever you embark on love play, you're wearing something nice—and something nice means either your birthday suit (plus, perhaps, a dab of perfume in one or two exciting places) or else whatever kind of sexy underwear or nightwear you know will excite your man. Bear in mind that though fashions change over the years, men remain fairly constant in their tastes. Your love play will probably be highly successful if you always dress for it in tiny lacy bras with lots of uplift, filmy or frilly pants (including some with split fronts), G-strings, old fashioned suspender-belts, transparent nighties and so on. In bed, men tend to prefer black above other colours, though red and white are quite popular. Do use your imagination and as with everything else, vary what you do and what you wear as much as possible. Let him believe there are many fascinating aspects to you, and always some yet to be discovered.

Finally, if all this talk about beautifying yourself for love play with your man seems to you to be so much male chauvinist exploitation of women, I suggest you look at the precisely similar advice I give to men in the previous chapter! Wives *and* husbands (however long they have been married) owe each other the compliment of making themselves as attractive as possible for the kind of bedroom romps we're about to describe.

The Techniques of Love Play

VERBAL TECHNIQUES. Just as a woman likes to be told that

she is beautiful and that she is loved, men also like to be complimented in bed. Even today, too many girls say next to nothing to their mates during love play, but they're missing out on a valuable bonus by keeping silent. It's amazing how just a quick word of encouragement will immediately increase your man's zest for love-making. So what are you going to say to him?

Telling him you love him is a good start of course. But you have to remember that a man's mind works in a very different way from yours. In sexual matters men tend to be far more basic than women and they are, on the whole, far less interested in the tender, romantic side of sexual attraction. So to turn your mate on, you usually have to say some pretty basic things to him.

First of all then compliment him on his body (however flabby and out of shape he is, he must have *some* good features!). Tell him you love the warmth of him, the strength of his muscles, the curve of his buttocks. Most of all, compliment him on his penis.

This kind of thing is of enormous psychological importance to a male. It's very hard for a woman to understand how a man's whole concept of his virility is bound up with his penis. He regards it as the embodiment of his maleness, the symbol of his potency. As you'll see if you read Chapter One: *How a Man is Made,* he tends to be quite ludicrously obsessed with the size of it, often failing to appreciate that it makes no particular difference to *you* whether his organ is large, medium or small.

So build up his ego. Tell him his penis is beautiful, magnificent, enormous, or whatever descriptions come into your head. Of course, the truth is that his organ is little different from anybody else's. Both of you realize that if it were lined up with a dozen others you might not even be able to pick it out from the rest, even if you've been married for 20 years!

It doesn't matter a bit that he knows you're talking with tongue in cheek. The more you can behave as though his penis were some sort of totem pole to be worshipped, the more he'll enjoy it, and you.

In your verbal love play, be as frank and as earthy as possible. It seems incredible nowadays, but for generations men and women were afraid to put names to each other's sex organs when they made love. Even today, there are many wives who do try to talk to their husbands in bed, but whose conversation is limited to such

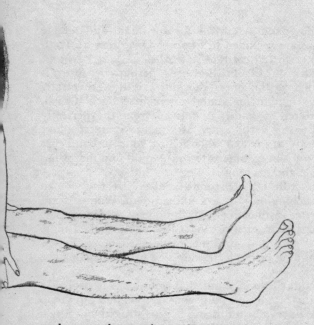

FIGURE 25

embarrassed remarks as 'Shall I rub your er . . . er . . . ?'

Remember love play is the time for being absolutely explicit, and for throwing off *all* your inhibitions. You'll find that it gives your man a great deal of pleasure if you cheerfully use words like 'penis' and 'vagina' as you caress each other.

Furthermore, most (though not all) men derive immense satisfaction from hearing their wives coming out with the so-called 'rude' words in bed. If you've never done this before, you'll probably be astonished at the effect you produce when you use the common Anglo-Saxon synonyms for the male and female organs. These terms are included in Chapter One: *How a Man is Made* and Chapter Two: *How a Woman is Made*.

As a rule the most erotic of all these words (perhaps because it is still widely regarded as the most 'shocking') is the universally known four-letter synonym for sexual intercourse 'fuck' which, you may be interested to know, is derived from the perfectly respectable Old English verb *fuggen*. If you use it during love play (and particularly at the end when telling your husband that the time has come for him to penetrate you), you'll find that it has immensely desirable and exciting results.

CARESSING HIS BODY. Fortunately, there are few women who need much teaching on how to cuddle a man. Women seem to have a much better instinct for the technique of tender caresses of the face and body than men do. As a rule the unskilled male neglects this part of love play, and tends to make a lunge for his partner's sex organs long before he has aroused her by stroking the rest of her body.

On the other hand, bear in mind that your man is probably much more genitally-orientated than you are. While you would very likely prefer to have your limbs and breasts stroked for quite a while before any approach is made to your sex organs, his main concern is usually to get you to caress his penis as soon as possible! So tantalize him for a minute or so if you like, tickling, stroking, squeezing and gently slapping his arms, chest, stomach, buttocks and thighs, but do not delay too long before you get to the area of his body where his primary interest lies.

CARESSING HIS PENIS. Don't feel that you should only grasp your husband's penis when you are both in bed. Quite a good way of initiating love play is simply to surprise him by unzipping his trousers and slipping your hand inside. Most men delight in being taken unawares like this. However, even today one comes across some men who are quite horrified at the idea of having anyone—even their wives—touch their penises, because they regard this as 'sinful masturbation'. A wife who is distressed by finding herself in this position should try to get her husband to see a doctor or marriage counsellor.

Stimulating the penis by hand isn't just something you learn overnight. It's quite a delicate and skilled art that will take you months or even years to master. You have one ally however, your husband. Most girls don't think of asking their menfolk exactly what they want done to their penises; how firmly they like to be held, how fast they like to be rubbed, and so on. Do bear in mind however that quite apart from his heterosexual experience, your mate (unless he is a very unusual man) probably started masturbation when he was about 12 or 13. In fact he's had time to become something of an expert on how a penis should be stimulated. So follow his advice on how he likes it done.

In general the mistakes that most inexperienced women make are:

(i) Not pressing firmly enough; you won't hurt him by even the firmest pressure, provided you apply it fairly gradually.

(ii) Not rubbing fast enough. A skilled wife can achieve a rate of 300-500 short up-and-down strokes each minute!

(iii) Using an awkward grip.

This last point is probably the most important of all. A girl who is in bed with a man for the first time will usually reach down (often with her left hand, which is of course less skilled then the right one anyway) and grasp his erect penis in her palm in the instinctive way shown in the top picture of figure 16. She can't

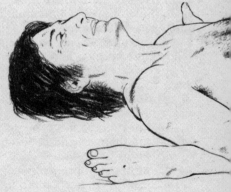

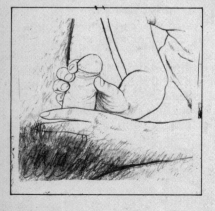

achieve any speed or sensitivity like this, and she's very likely to produce jerky, irregular movements that hurt the poor man's organ rather than stimulate it.

It's much better to reach down and place the right hand in the position shown in the middle picture, with the thumb nearest the husband's tummy and the pads of the fingers on the far side of his penis. Up-and-down strokes (anything from half an inch to three inches in extent, depending on his preference) will now produce a most desirable effect on your man. Simple squeezing between finger and thumb is also very popular.

Even more effective (and particularly valuable if the husband's potency is flagging a little) is reversing the hand, so that the wife's fingers are on the side of the penis nearest the husband's tummy, while her thumb is on the curved side. To take up this grip really effectively, she should sit or kneel facing him, between his legs— as shown in the bottom picture. While positioned like this, it's very easy for her to use her left hand when the right one needs a rest, or to use both together at times.

These are the basic grips, but there are literally thousands of other ways of using your hands to stimulate your man's penis— for instance, holding it between the flats of your hands and rolling it to and fro; stroking the tip (the glans) with the pads of your fingers; flicking the frenulum, which is the part on the curved side (furthest from the stomach when erect) that stands out like a bow-string; pulling the penis forward as far as it will go and then letting it spring back so that its tip rubs along your palm, your breasts, or even the sheet; and so on as far as your imagination will extend.

In fact, the best thing is to be as inventive as possible—try everything, and see just how much you can discover between you.

Apart from using your hands, you can also stimulate your mate's penis with almost any other part of your body. The breasts are ideal for this purpose. Try resting his organ between them and squeezing them together. At the same time, you can either stroke his penis with your finger tips or bend your head forward so that you can lick the tip with your tongue.

Many women become quite skilled at stimulating their menfolk with their hair or by putting the penis in the armpit. In fact, any nook or cranny of your body will do for this purpose—it's a case of whatever turns you both on. Putting the man's penis between the woman's buttocks is also quite popular, but you should bear in mind that your bottom isn't the most germ-free area of your body, which means that if your husband does this he should wash his penis before entering your vagina.

USING YOUR MOUTH. Most women don't have to be told how to kiss a man on the lips, but don't forget the adventurous kisses: putting your tongue in his mouth, as well as accepting his in yours, kissing with mouths wide open, gently biting his lips, and so on.

Furthermore, your mouth was made for kissing his entire body, so don't stop at his lips. Kiss his neck, his chest, his nipples, his arms and his stomach, nuzzling, licking and sinking your teeth into the muscular parts of his body.

Most of all, kiss his penis. Oral sex is one of the most delightful aspects of love, and immensely satisfying to both partners. I doubt if many of the readers of this book will have serious inhibitions about mouth-genital contact, but since I still come across women who think that their husbands are being 'dirty' by asking them to do this kind of thing, let me say that this is a completely healthy and natural activity which has greatly enriched

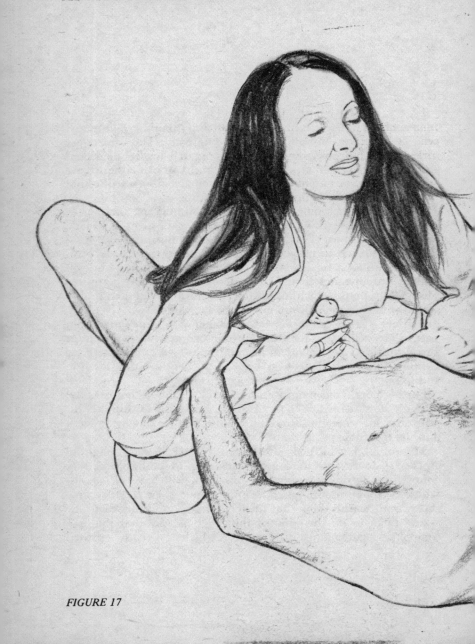

FIGURE 17

many marriages. Incidentally, a very large number of the men who go to call girls and prostitutes do so mainly because these girls, unlike their wives, have no inhibitions about putting a penis to their lips.

If you've never had any kind of oral sex before, you can simply begin by holding your husband's penis and applying kiss after kiss to the tip (the glans).

Next, try the experiment of gently taking the tip in your mouth and rocking forwards and backwards. Alternate this with licking the glans, just as you would an ice cream cone. In fact, a few rather exotically-minded couples do even go in for putting dollops of ice cream, whipped cream or jam on the end of the husband's penis so that the wife can lick it up!

That's all there really is to oral sex—the mysterious activity about which self-appointed moralists have made such a fuss in the past; the completely natural way of expressing love that still carries the risk of a heavy jail sentence for both husband and wife

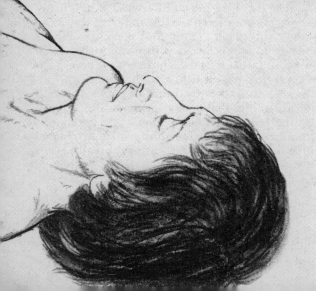

in some states of the USA.

Of course you'll find ways of refining these techniques as time goes by. Swirling your tongue round your husband's penis while it is inside your mouth (the so-called 'silken-swirl') is quite effective. So too is using your tongue to flick the taut bowstring-like frenulum on the curved side of the penis. You can combine mouth and breast stimulation by placing your man's penis between your breasts (as shown in figure 17) and leaning forward to lick, suck or kiss it. Or you can simply kneel on the floor at your husband's feet while he thrusts his penis in and out.

Best of all, you can let your husband excite your clitoris and vagina with his mouth while you are kissing his genitals. Convenient positions for this kind of mutual stimulation are discussed at the end of the previous chapter under the heading CUNNILINGUS, which is the medical word for kissing the vagina and vulva (kissing the penis is called fellatio).

There are only two problems about taking a penis in your mouth. The first is that excessive penetration does worry many women. A man approaches your mouth in just the same way as he does your vagina—he wants to get as far into it as possible. So it's sometimes hard for him to appreciate that thrusting six or seven inches of penis down your throat may half choke you! Where this is happening you've got to make it clear to him that he has to consider *your* feelings as well as his own, and that he ought to take it easy when you indicate to him that enough is enough.

Secondly, there's the problem of ejaculation. A lot of couples will quite often continue with oral sex until the man reaches his climax. The difficulty is that while the husband usually wants to come inside his wife's mouth, many women dislike the idea of swallowing seminal fluid, though others are more than happy to do so.

The fluid is actually completely harmless (and can't cause pregnancy by this route, as some people imagine) but if you find it a bit messy the best thing to do is simply to wait for 10 seconds or so and then discreetly deposit it in a hanky kept under the pillow. Some couples use a French letter during fellatio, but most people would find this a very clinical way of making love.

You can of course pull away at the last second, but this is perhaps a trifle unkind to your husband—a bit like the practice of *coitus interruptus*, or withdrawal, (see Chapter Ten: *How to Prevent Babies*) which a lot of people still unwisely use as a means of contraception.

However if you feel you must take your man's penis out of your mouth before orgasm, do your best to offer him something else instead so as not to spoil his moment of ecstasy. As he comes out, you could take him in your hand and rub furiously for the last few seconds. Or you could swing your body across his, and thrust him into your vagina.

Alternatively, you could let him reach his climax over your breasts or any other part of your body. Most men find this very exciting, particularly if the light is on so that they can see what is happening.

OTHER TECHNIQUES OF LOVE PLAY. I can't overstress the fact that any activity you both enjoy in bed is OK, with only one or two exceptions (see Chapter Nine: *Is There Anything Wrong with Doing This, Doctor?*). So whatever ways you can think of to excite your husband (or that he can suggest to you), try them out. Here are a few more suggestions to stimulate your imagination:

Stroke, kiss and tickle his testicles (his balls). Though this isn't as exciting to him as doing the same thing to his penis would be (it won't normally bring him to orgasm, for instance), he'll find it very nice. Do be wary though. His testicles are the most pain-sensitive organs of his body, so you mustn't get carried away and squeeze hard! If you take one of them in your mouth (as many women do), treat it as carefully as you would an egg, and if your mate starts making a strange squealing noise, *don't* assume that it's pleasure: let go!

You can also stimulate your husband's perineum—this is the area of skin underneath his body, immediately behind the testicles and in front of his bottom. Use your fingers, your lips or your tongue for this.

There is no reason why you shouldn't caress his bottom as well (*postillionage*). Many men find this very exciting, especially while the penis is being stimulated at the same time. Do be careful where you put your fingers afterwards however, bearing in mind what we said earlier in the chapter about the anus not being the most germ-free area of the body.

You'll find quite a lot of other ideas in the chapter on slightly unusual sex activities (Chapter Nine: *Is There Anything Wrong with Doing This, Doctor?*), but you'll find that it will take you many months or even years of intensive practice to become really skilled at the basic techniques outlined in this chapter. So go to it ladies—make bedtime great fun for your husbands, and for yourselves.

CHAPTER EIGHT
The Positions of Love

Sex is not likely to remain very interesting for a couple who, during the course of 40 years or so, always make love in the same position. It's traditionally said that men need variety in love-making, but the truth is that women do too. It's very easy for sex to become rather dull and boring after a few years of marriage unless both partners are willing to experiment and innovate with love play, and to try out new positions of intercourse.

Variations in position don't just produce psychological benefits. They also alter the angle at which the penis enters the vagina, and so create all sorts of new pressures on the male and female organs, thereby causing unusual and pleasant *physical* sensations for both husband and wife. So all the various positions are definitely worth trying.

How many of them are there? All over the world are people who will assure you that there are x positions of intercourse— some say that it is 123, some mention a figure of 84, while others confidently claim that it is 513. There are even people who believe fervently that the number is 69[1]—an obvious confusion with the '69' technique of love play (described in Chapter Six: *How to Handle a Woman*).

In fact, the truth is that there is *no* definite total number of positions of intercourse. The reason for this is quite simple—*how do you define a position?* If you choose to buy one of those expensive books that claim to illustrate hundreds of different postures, you'll find that number 331 differs from number 332 only by the bending of a knee or an elbow, or perhaps because the hair is combed backward rather than forward. To call these 'different positions' is frankly ludicrous.

There is really no point in going into finicky details (which any sensible couple can work out for themselves anyway). Nor,

---

[1]*See the penultimate page of Ian Fleming's* From Russia with Love.

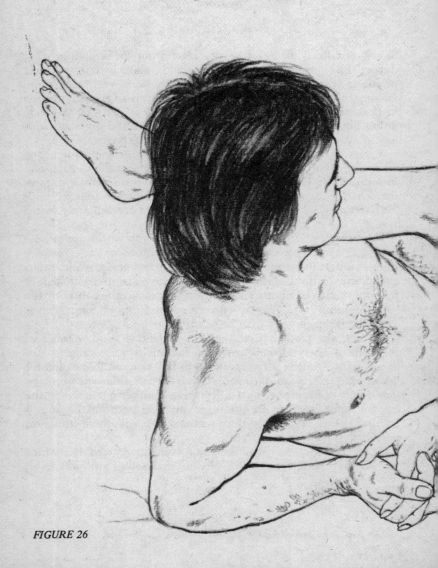

FIGURE 26

I think, is there any value in describing positions which could be achieved only by trained acrobats or contortionists. Quite obviously, a Russian lady gymnast could manage some quite extraordinary postures in combination with a double-jointed male escapologist, but these sort of antics are not likely to be of the least use to the average couple who only want to bring some extra fun and variety into their love-making.

So, what we'll do is describe the basic positions of love in three sections (Face-to-Face, Rear Entry, and Side positions) and to mention the more important variations. You and your partner will almost certainly think of refinements for yourselves and should have tremendous fun in discovering them.

Face-to-Face Positions

MAN ABOVE, WOMAN BENEATH. This is without doubt the commonest group of intercourse positions, if only because there are still so many people (particularly those who haven't had the opportunity to have much sex education) who think that any other way of having sex is 'rude'.

Most frequently, the woman lies flat on her back with her knees bent (as in figure 18 on page 46) so that the soles of her feet are on the bed. This is the famous 'missionary' position, so called because scandalized Victorian preachers are alleged to have forbidden the other more uninhibited postures that members of their flocks chose for love-making. (One wonders how the missionaries *knew*.)

The missionary position is certainly quite a good one, and it does allow the man's pubic bone to 'grind' against the woman's, which is important for reasons outlined in Chapter Two: *How a Woman is Made*. As with all the face-to-face positions however, it's a bit difficult for the husband to stimulate the wife's breasts or (more particularly) her clitoris with his fingers.

Variation 1. The first and simplest variation is for the woman just to straighten her legs and to spread them wide on the bed. Entry is a little more difficult with the legs like this, and the sensation produced is only slightly (if at all) different from that felt in the basic position.

Variation 2. The man lies with his legs outside the woman's (as in figure 19 on page 56). His thighs squeeze hers together, and her thighs compress his penis. For that reason, this technique is useful if the woman's vagina has been made loose by childbirth. However this is a situation which can be improved. Try the exercises described in Chapter Two : *How a Woman is Made*, in order to tighten things up.

Variation 3. The woman brings her legs up over the man's hips or waist (as in figure 20 on page 72). This alters the tilt of her pelvis and so gives very good penetration of her vagina. She can, if she wishes, cross her legs round his middle, so increasing the sense of closeness. There is, by the way, a myth among some people to the effect that a woman who crosses her legs during love-making can injure or even kill her partner. I well remember the first time this dread warning was passed on to me in the school playground! Fortunately, it turned out to be complete nonsense, like so much of the rest of the information that young people give each other when no proper sex education is available at school.

Variation 4. This variation is merely an extension of the last one, but you need to be more supple. The woman draws her legs even further up so that she can hook them over her mate's shoulders (as shown in figure 21 on page 82). This gives very deep penetration indeed, so it's important that entry should be *gentle*.

Don't start intercourse with this position (or any of the other deep-penetration postures). It's much better to begin with something else and, if you wish, work up to deep penetration after 10, 20 or even 30 minutes when the vagina has had time to really relax.

Variation 5. Using a pillow. In any of the above positions, you can produce subtle alterations in the depth and angle of penetration by simply putting a pillow (two for advanced lovers) under the lady's bottom. This usually works best when she has her legs in the air, as in Variation 3 above.

Variation 6. Split levels. The last three techniques we have mentioned also work very well if the two partners are on different levels, e.g. if the wife is lying back on the edge of the bed while the husband kneels on the floor (as shown in figure 22 on page 90). An inventive couple can think of several such situations—for example, with the wife sitting in a chair, or perhaps lying back on a high couch while the husband stands between her legs.

WOMAN ABOVE, MAN BENEATH. This range of positions is very useful, particularly when (as is so often the case) there's a big difference in the weights of husband and wife. Let's face it, no matter how enthusiastic one is about the missionary position and its variations, they're not always a lot of fun for a 100lb. woman who's gasping for breath beneath a 200lb. husband.

So, many couples quite often make love with the man lying flat on his back and the woman lying on top of him. (Figure 23 on page 94.) Her legs can be inside or outside his—the former position gives her an opportunity to exert pressure on his penis with her thighs.

Until quite recently, it was said that this position was psychologically harmful to a man, because it 'diminished his role as the master!' In these days of Women's Lib., I think that this can be regarded as sheer bunkum. Certainly, I have never known a man who has suffered emotional harm from using the position. Perhaps a more pertinent argument is that it does sometimes tend to induce a certain laziness in the male—a 'let *her* make love to *me*' attitude. This is well illustrated by the story (current in British hospitals) of a young lady surgeon who became pregnant. When asked who the father was she replied that it was someone who had slipped into her hospital room late one night; the only thing she knew for sure was that it was a Consultant.

'Why a Consultant?'

'Why?' replied the young doctor coolly, 'because he made me do all the work, of course!'

Variation 1. The woman simply raises the top part of her body on outstretched arms so that her husband can see and feel her breasts, which is exciting for them both.

Variation 2. The 'frog position'. The woman places the soles of her feet on the upper surfaces of the man's feet and both of them spread their legs wide apart with knees bent (in much the same attitude as that of a frog's legs). Their lower limbs are now in close and intimate contact all the way down, and this enables them to 'work together' in a most agreeable way during intercourse.

Variation 3. The woman kneels astride the man's hips as shown in figure 24 on page 111. This position is very useful when a husband is having trouble with his potency or his control. For the reasons why, see Chapter Eleven : *Problems with Sex*. Like the next variation, it's also very good in pregnancy.

Variation 4. Very similar to No 3 except that the wife sits on her husband's penis with her legs stretched out on either side of

FIGURE 27

his chest or over his shoulders (see figure 25 on page 114). She can then bump up and down in the movement that the French so aptly describe as 'the Lyon stagecoach'. Or, if she likes, she can turn a complete circle while still sitting on her husband, so that naturally his penis also rotates through 360 degrees inside her vagina.

Variation 5. The 'X-position'. While sitting on her husband as in variation 4, the woman leans completely backwards until she is flat on the bed. Because considerable pressure is put on the penis, it tends to 'pop out' unless the couple take things very gently. Once the position is achieved, the penis presses very hard on the woman's bladder, so unless she has remembered to empty it first, there may be slightly hilarious results when she reaches her orgasm.

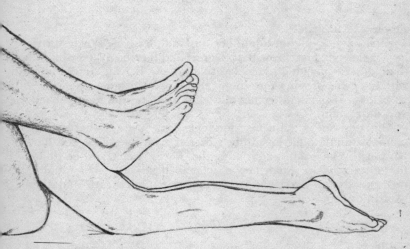

In practice, this variation is often more comfortable and satisfying if the man puts one of his legs across the woman's thigh as in figure 26 on page 128. Note that the couple are holding hands, which is not only romantic but which helps them to pull the male organ more deeply into the female one.

(Note for advanced lovers: this is really a *flanquette* position—see the last part of this chapter.

Variation 6. This starts off rather like variation 3, with the woman kneeling astride the man's penis—but now he draws his legs up and wraps them round her body (like the man in figure 27 above). He then uses his legs to tug himself up repeatedly into her vagina, a rather exotic procedure which can give both partners a pleasantly wild and abandoned feeling.

Warning: this one is really only for men who are reasonably

supple and athletic!

Variation 7. Lying on top of her husband, the wife slowly turns her whole body first through 45 degrees and then 90 degrees (more than this is difficult to achieve) so that she is lying across him with his penis pressing into the side wall of her vagina (see figure 28 below). If the penis comes out while you are rotating, go back and start again.

This position is quite nice for long, lazy love. It enables the man to stimulate his loved one's breasts with one hand and her bottom (by love slaps, etc.) with the other. It can also be done the other way up, (man above, woman beneath) but is usually rather easier as described, with the man underneath and the woman on top.

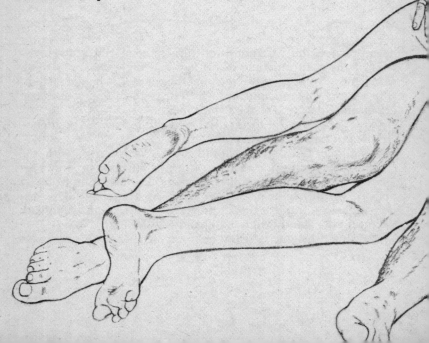

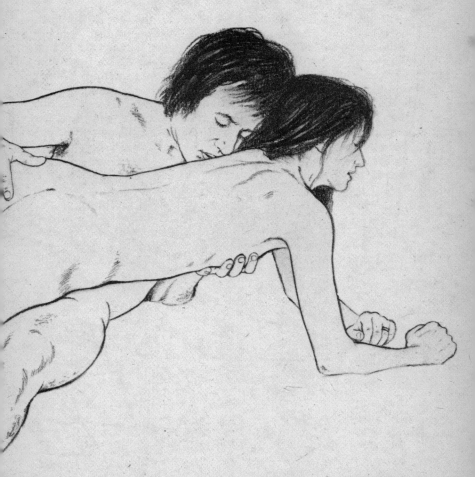

FIGURE 28

Variation 8. Just like variation 3, except that the husband sits on a chair (as shown in figure 29 on page 138) with his wife astride him.

BOTH PARTNERS STANDING. Face-to-face love-making in a standing position is very common, because unmarried people sometimes have nowhere to make love except up against a wall. Intercourse in these inauspicious circumstances is usually hurried, awkward and unsatisfactory, partly because most men are a good deal taller than most women. Only the Napoleon and Josephine couples of this world can achieve a reasonably comfortable entry in a face-to-face standing position. Some people in this unfortunate situation try to get round the problem by standing the lady on a couple of bricks—but there is the ever-present danger that she may fall off half-way through and thus shatter what little romantic atmosphere there is about this way of having intercourse.

But making love standing face-to-face in the bedroom without the encumbrance of clothes is a quite different matter and can be great fun. The wife will often need a firm stool (a foot stool is ideal) to stand on, unless she is taller than her partner, and she should lean against a wall for support, bracing herself against the man's thrusts.

Variation 1. This is only for young, lusty husbands with strong backs! The man picks up his wife, around the waist or by the buttocks, and lifts her into the air. She wraps her arms round his neck and her legs round his body (as in figure 30 on page 141) and rocks vigorously to-and-fro.

Variation 2. Much the same but even more acrobatic. The wife leans right back until her head and hands are on the floor, while her legs remain wrapped round her husband's body. Few men have the strength to manage this for more than a minute or so

FIGURE 29

(so orgasm is rarely reached) but the position certainly provides quite an amusing interlude during love-making.

Variation 3. Making love on the stairs can be a very good way of getting round the problem of difference in height between man and woman.

FACE-TO-FACE: LYING ON SIDE. This is the final face-to-face position. It makes entry a bit difficult, but once in, it's pleasant and agreeable for long slow love-making interspersed with conversation. It's nice for couples who want to go to sleep afterwards with their sex organs still joined together. But advanced lovers will usually prefer one of the *flanquette* positions described at the end of this chapter.

Rear Entry Positions

A great deal of criticism has been flung at those who use these love positions by 'moralists' in years gone by, mainly because they associated the idea of rear entry with the way that 'brute beasts of the field' (to quote the marriage service) have intercourse. These methods were also supposed to be favoured by allegedly 'inferior' races and were therefore deemed not suitable for civilized Europeans. (See the note about the 'missionary position' earlier in the chapter). Even today, the first position we are about to describe is sometimes known as coitus *à la négresse*, though in fact negro girls do not seem to have any special predilection for this position.

WOMAN BENEATH, MAN ABOVE. Basically, what happens here is that the wife kneels on the bed with her head well down, as in figure 31 on page 143. Her husband kneels behind her and gently enters her vagina, with one or other of them using a hand in front of the vulva to steer the penis in (you may have to keep it there throughout). As with all the other rear entry positions,

FIGURE 30

FIGURE 31

this position gives the man an ideal opportunity to stimulate the woman's breasts and, of course, her clitoris with his finger tips.

Variation 1. Instead of kneeling, the woman lies flat on her face on the bed with legs apart. This makes entry a bit difficult, but the wife can help the penis in with her hand.

Variation 2. Instead of kneeling *between* the girl's legs, the man places his knees on either side of her. Then he *slowly and gradually*

eases forward until he is virtually sitting astride her back and
'riding' her. This is an advanced technique and should not be
rushed; it may be uncomfortable and completely unsuccessful if
the wife has not been prepared and stimulated by careful love
play.

Variation 3. Split levels. The wife lies face down with legs apart
on the edge of the bed while the husband kneels behind her.

Variation 4. Very similar, but the husband grasps his wife's thighs and then stands up, so that he is holding her rather as in a child's 'wheelbarrow' game.

MAN BENEATH, WOMAN ABOVE. This variety of rear-entry position is not of quite such value. However many men do like to lie flat on their backs with their wives (also face upwards) on top of them. Almost invariably the husband or wife's hand has to be placed in front of the vulva to keep the penis from popping out. Some women do find that the use of this position gives them a very 'abandoned' sensation, and that they achieve quite an unusually intense climax as a result.

Variation 1. It's very pleasant if the man lies flat on his back and the woman just sits on his penis while facing away from him. By altering the angle to which she leans forward she can produce agreeable variations in the sensations she experiences. If she wishes, she can gradually lower her head until her face is on the sheets between her husband's legs.

Variation 2. Much the same as variation 1, but with the man sitting up as well, as shown in figure 32 on page 145.

Variation 3. The same thing, but with the man sitting on a chair instead of on the bed.

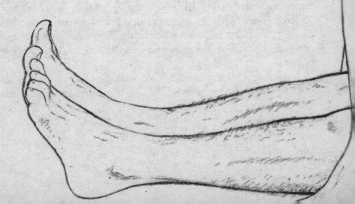

FIGURE 32

REAR ENTRY STANDING. This is a very nice way of making love, and easier than face-to-face standing intercourse. The wife bends over so as to reveal the exciting sight of her vulva between her thighs. She can, if she wishes, lean against a chair or, preferably, a more solid structure such as a chest of drawers as chairs tend to get knocked over as things become more hectic toward the end.

Variation 1. The wife stands upright instead of bending over. Entry is not so easy this way, but the man can more readily caress his loved one's breasts, kiss her neck and murmur sweet nothings in her ear.

Variation 2. The wife bends forward until her hands are on the floor, and then her husband helps her to wrap her legs around his body. This position again is really for athletes only, and the man should bear in mind that the girl will *not* enjoy having her face rammed repeatedly into the carpet! A very large feather cushion under her arms may be helpful.

REAR ENTRY, BOTH ON SIDE. Intercourse with both husband and wife lying on their sides (her bottom tucked cosily up against the lower part of his tummy) can be very satisfying. As with the corresponding face-to-face love-making position, it's possible for both partners to fall asleep after orgasm with their genitals still in contact—an advantage which many couples value.

Variation 1. The wife leans forward so that the top half of her body is at right angles to the man's. This produces an interesting change in sensation in the vagina and in the penis. If he wants to, the man can increase the effect by gently leaning backwards. This does, however, make communication between the lovers rather difficult!

Variation 2. As for variation 1, but the wife moves one of her legs back (either *between* the husband's legs or *above* them) until it is in a straight line with the top half of her body. By subtle alterations in leg position she can produce all sorts of interesting effects for both partners.

Flank Positions

I use this phrase to cover all positions in which the man is 'sideways on' to the woman. Relatively few couples seem to have discovered these refinements for themselves, but they are well worth experimenting with as you become more skilled in love-making. Virtually all of them are especially useful in pregnancy at the time when the woman's tummy starts to get in the way of rather more orthodox positions. There are three groups of positions— 'straight' sideways, *cuissade*, and *flanquette*.

'STRAIGHT' SIDEWAYS. The basic way of doing this is for the woman to lie flat on her back with her knees bent or (if she prefers it) her legs in the air. Her man lies on his side, with the lower part of his body curled under her bottom so that her legs are across his thighs. This very comfortable position is shown in figure 33 on page 148.

Variation 1. The man lies flat on his back on the bed while his wife sits across his thighs. This is not so comfortable, but may be chosen as a change.

Variation 2. This is virtually the same thing but with *both* partners sitting. The man is usually settled on a comfortable chair with the girl seated across his lap so that his penis comes up between her thighs and enters her vulva. Some couples take pleasure in doing this with their clothes on, (apart, of course, from the lady's panties) thereby adding a spice of 'naughtiness' to the procedure. Indeed, a few husbands and wives do enjoy the 'risk' of surreptitiously making love in this way (under cover

FIGURE 33

of the girl's skirts) in relatively open situations.

CUISSADE POSITIONS. This French term simply means that the man takes his wife from a half-rear and half-sideways angle—in other words, he enters her from behind, but with one of his legs through hers. This is easier to explain with a picture than to describe, so look at figure 34 on page 164.

Cuissade positions allow the penis to enter the vagina at all sorts of interesting angles and (if the man lies back at right angles to the woman) to a remarkable depth. Instead of describing them all in minute detail, I think it's best if we leave you to experiment with these interesting and exciting variations for yourself.

FLANQUETTE POSITIONS. This is another French term which simply describes the side positions in which the entry is 'half-facing', rather than 'half-rear'. In other words, the husband is face-to-face with his wife but with his leg thrust between hers. Look at figure 35 on page 198 which makes this clear.

There are many *flanquette* positions for you to discover for

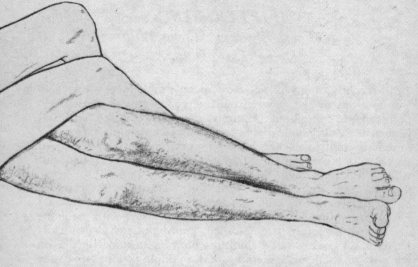

yourselves, but they're all nice and they all allow very good penetration, usually combined with pressure on the clitoris by the man's thigh. One word of warning—the fact that the woman's leg is between the man's thighs renders him vulnerable to a very obvious injury. So whatever happens, ladies, *do* be careful not to bring your knee up suddenly!

Final Note

Be wary of trying the more exotic positions if you're doubtful whether you're physically fit enough for them. Husbands or wives who have disc trouble or similar back problems would obviously be very unwise to attempt the few positions that put a strain on the spine.

Finally, remember that a knowledge of the 40 or so positions we've described here does *not* make you an expert lover—far from it. Anyone who has read this chapter before mastering the basic arts of love play and before finding out all about the anatomy of love should go back to Page One and start afresh.

CHAPTER NINE
Is There Anything Wrong With Doing This, Doctor?

Until recently, many (if not most) people thought that anything a couple did in bed (apart from intercourse in the 'missionary' position) was 'perverted'. Happily, there are now few men and women who take such a view—but the fact remains that many husbands and wives are basically very unsure about various practices that they, or their partners, feel like trying in bed, but which they think might be 'kinky'.

That's why people send in endless questions to advice columns enquiring whether this or that is *wrong*. Now, in my answers I always try to make it clear that I am concerned with medicine and not with morals. If a so-called 'kinky' practice is medically harmful I'll say so—but I think it would be an impertinence on my part to condemn something that a couple do in the privacy of their bedroom as being morally wrong. Unlike many commentators on sexual matters in the past, I see no reason to start labelling people as depraved or disgusting because they happen to find mutual pleasure in something that is of no interest to me personally.

So in this chapter we'll look at various common bedroom activities, judging them on only two criteria—whether they are likely to enrich a marriage, and whether they could do any medical harm to the couple involved.

Is oral love-play OK?
Perfectly—'mouth music', as it's sometimes called, is one of the nicest aids to marital happiness. You'll find details of the various techniques in Chapters Six and Seven (*How to Handle a Woman* and *How to Handle a Man*), but people still seem to get in a bit of a state about oral sex, behaving as if it were something terribly vulgar or indecent. I've even encountered men and women who thought it caused cancer of the throat, which seems

a trifle irrational to say the least.

I would give one commonsense warning about these techniques : obviously it's rather silly to indulge in oral love play when you have an infection of either the mouth area or the genital region. In practice, it's rare for germs to be carried to the sex organs from the mouth but it can happen, just as ordinary kissing can transmit cold germs from one mouth to another.

Perhaps what is more important, genital infections like thrush, gonorrhoea or syphilis can occasionally be transferred to the lips, tongue or throat by oral/genital contact. So if you have any kind of discharge or genital sore, don't have sex (oral or otherwise) until the cause has been diagnosed. (See Chapter Twelve : *Trouble Down Below*.) Neglect of this simple and fairly obvious health principle has led to people getting such bizarre conditions as gonorrhoea of the tonsils—which may sound rather funny, but which is no joke when you've got it.

Is blowing down the penis harmful?

Yes, it could well be. This practice has become popular in some areas (particularly in the USA) but it's most unwise. There's a chance that the wife who blows down her husband's penis may damage his sexual equipment, temporarily or permanently.

Is it all right if the wife swallows the seminal fluid?

This is a very commonly asked question. As I've said in Chapter Seven, many women are disgusted by the idea of swallowing the fluid anyway, though others take the view of Molly Bloom in James Joyce's *Ulysses* and derive a lot of satisfaction from it.

Seminal fluid is quite harmless and non-toxic but it has one possible side-effect that I ought to point out. A woman who is more than seven months pregnant should *not* swallow it in case it puts her into premature labour. African tribes use a draught made from the fluid to try to bring women into labour, and I understand from Professor S. M. M. Karim, who is currently the world's leading authority on prostaglandins (which are very potent chemicals present in certain body tissues) that it would theoretically be possible for the amount of prostaglandins in a single ejaculate to have this effect. However, he says that there is no danger at all during the first six months of pregnancy.

Is it all right to put things in the vagina?
That depends on what you're going to put in—and how easy it is to get out! Any casualty officer soon learns that a lot of people have the habit of popping all sorts of daft things inside during love-making. For instance, very often a husband and wife will go out together on a Saturday night, have perhaps a few too many drinks, and then return home for some rather tipsy love-making. Suddenly it strikes one or other of them as a good joke to pop, say, an apple inside the vagina. The joke wears a bit thin when they discover they can't get it out again! So the wife goes along to the nearest hospital with some incredible story about having tripped over a fruit bowl, which the doctor listens to with some cynicism.

The object can always be removed, but the woman may need a general anaesthetic first. So my advice would be *never* to put anything into the vagina that wasn't specifically designed for it, and above all to avoid sharp or breakable objects. In the past I have had considerable difficulty in removing fragile bottles of make-up or perfume which no-one in their right mind should want inserted into their bodies.

It's quite all right to put in contraceptive pessaries, however, and in many parts of the world (notably West Africa), husbands encourage their wives to get certain effervescent brands from the clinic because of the pleasant tingle they produce for both partners.

I have also had a number of letters from couples who pop an ice cube in just before love-making in order to produce the same effect. Provided the cube is very small and not too cold (so that it melts within about 30 seconds) I would say that as an occasional practice this would probably be harmless. At least an ice cube has the merit of vanishing by itself, which is more than one can say for many of the other dotty things that people put into themselves.

But what about inserting vibrators?
Well, that's a different matter, because vibrators are meant to be placed in the vagina, and those made by reputable manufacturers shouldn't (in theory) break or have bits fall off them when they're inside.

I would caution, however, against the use of *rectal* vibrators. These devices have become very popular in some countries (especially in Scandinavia) in recent years, but the danger of them is that *they can get lost*. Despite its French name (*le cul*), the back passage isn't a *cul de sac* like the vagina, and there have been a number of unfortunate and embarrassing cases in which men and women who have used these things have ended up having to undergo an abdominal operation to have them removed from somewhere in the region of their livers—very nasty.

But what about electric vibrators generally? Are they OK?
Well yes, they're quite harmless things, though it's important to ensure that those which run off the mains, rather than a battery, are properly earthed. When they first appeared in the shops some years ago a lot of people were offended by them and thought them 'obscene'. This is why they still tend to be advertised (in the most respectable journals!) as being for general massage ('the

revitalization of those tired tissues' as one advertisement felicitously puts it). But, as I think nearly everyone knows by now, most of the millions of vibrators that have been sold in recent years are intended (and used) purely as sex aids.

Now there's nothing medically wrong with this, provided that a couple don't expect that a vibrator will be some kind of magic remedy to any sexual difficulties they may have, though some patients who are 'frigid' may well derive some help from the use of a vibrator (see Chapter Eleven). If a couple buy one just to add to their bedroom fun, that's fine.

The most commonly used type of vibrator, shown in figure 36, is made of plastic and was quite obviously designed by a man. It is, as you can see, penis-shaped, hard, cold and unyielding. It also makes a devil of a racket, so that anyone who lives in a house with thin walls would be well advised to use it only when the neighbours are out!

Happily, more romantic-looking (and quieter) vibrators are slowly coming onto the market. They can be placed in the vagina, on the penis, or (most commonly) over the area of the clitoris, where of course they have the greatest effect. Some types can be strapped to the back of the husband's hand; if he then places the tips of his fingers on the wife's clitoris the transmitted vibration will give her quite an agreeable and unusual sensation.

Most women could reach a climax by using a vibrator, though I would stress, however, that few wives regard the feeling produced by a vibrator as being anything like as good as 'the real thing'.

Are clitoral stimulators safe to use?
Yes, though as I explained in Chapter Two quite frankly I don't think they're of much value as sex aids.

Basically, these devices are just rubber rings which fit round the base of the penis. As you can see from the picture of a typical model (figure 37) there's always a projection of some sort on the top surface, and this is supposed to rub against the wife's clitoris during intercourse and so excite her.

If you go into the shops where these often rather over-priced objects are sold, you may well be approached by ladies who will discreetly whisper a great deal of pseudo-scientific nonsense about them in your ear. They will talk knowledgeably about how the stimulators are essential for the woman with a 'high clitoris' or a 'hidden clitoris'. Pay no attention to all this bunkum—the idea of a high or hidden clitoris is a myth that was exploded long years ago. A woman who doesn't respond sexually has problems in her mind, not her clitoris—see Chapter Eleven.

If you want to buy one of the stimulators for fun, go right ahead. But bear in mind that quite a lot of women do find them uncomfortable (if not actually painful)—so don't be disappointed if your purchase fails to do all that the saleslady claimed for it.

Does the same apply to the 'textured condoms' that sex shops sell?

More or less. These gaily-coloured sheaths with projections

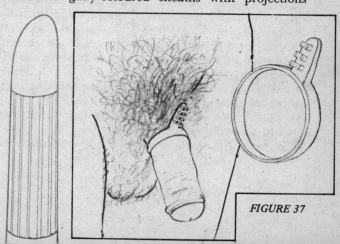

FIGURE 36

FIGURE 37

sticking out all over them are supposed to produce increased stimulation of the vagina, but I think that (once again) the designers have rather misunderstood the nature of female sexuality. Most women are merely amused, rather than excited, by seeing a man looking (as one of my correspondents put it) 'like a randy sea anemone'. However if the devices produce a bit of fun in the bedroom, then that's fine.

One word of warning—at the present time, most textured sheathes are *not* designed to act as contraceptives, and responsible manufacturers will state this fact on the packet.

Don't some people actually put things inside the penis?
Yes they do—and a very foolish and dangerous practice it is. I've dealt in Chapter Two with the folly of putting things into the female urinary passage (the urethra), and the same objections apply in the male. Anything you push into the 'pipe' could cause an infection and may get lost—or stuck. I well remember an unfortunate man whose wife, in a moment of over-enthusiasm, had put the stem of a flower down his penis. This doubtless looked very attractive to her, but trouble arose when the time came to remove it—the flower head came off in her hand! Because the tiny leaves on the stem pointed *upward*, the plant (which had gone in easily) was now completely jammed, and a trip to the operating theatre was necessary in order to get it out. I don't think the couple will be experimenting with that particular kind of flower power again.

Is there anything wrong with using exciting pictures in the bedroom to add spice to lovemaking?
Not at all, though these will probably appeal more to the husband than to the wife. In some countries this sort of practice is very widespread : Japanese couples, for instance, often have lavishly-

illustrated 'pillow books' to aid their lovemaking and I believe that *Playboy* magazine often fulfils a similar role in the USA. There is nothing 'dirty' or 'pornographic' about this—it's just another example of how anything that is harmless and fun and mutually satisfying can enrich a couple's relationship.

Some people, for instance, like to take things a step further and put large mirrors by the bed (or even on the ceiling) so that they can watch themselves making love. Once again, if you enjoy it then by all means do it, and *don't* let any self-appointed moralists make you feel embarrassed or ashamed about it.

Doesn't the use of sexy pictures and mirrors encourage people to have fantasies about other partners?

Well, what if it does? People are only human and there's no doubt that during intercourse husbands (and many wives) will sometimes drift off into a pleasant reverie about making love to some other person. Such flights of imagination are usually preferable to the risk of actual infidelity. And if (as is often the case) a spot of fantasy makes the husband or wife a better lover, then this is all to the good.

Some couples find it mutually stimulating to verbalise their fantasies, or to act out roles. If you and your partner find this entertaining then it will certainly add variety to your love-making as well as giving you glimpses of your partner's mind and imagination you might otherwise miss.

What about wife-swapping?

This is a very difficult one. Wife-swapping and the holding of orgies have definitely become much commoner in recent years. I think a couple who are considering going in for this have got to consider very seriously for themselves whether their emotions (and particularly the wife's emotions) are going to be able to stand the stresses that such activities will probably produce.

On a more physical level, it's important to bear in mind that an orgy is an ideal place to get an infection. VD is pretty common in all levels of society these days and it only needs one person with unsuspected gonorrhoea (a disease which may produce *no* symptoms, especially in the female) to infect a whole roomful of people.

And of course, far commoner than VD are the 'minor' infections like thrush and trichomonas ('TV'). I would hazard a guess that nowadays the majority of younger women acquire one of these 'bugs' at some time or other.[1] Put an infected girl in an orgy situation and most of the participants will be going home with thrush or 'TV' in their genital tracts. Indeed, I believe that the activities of quite a few wife-swapping groups have ground to a halt as a result of outbreaks of these painful and irritating infections.

Can anything be done about men who want to have intercourse in the presence of fetish objects (leatherwear, rubberwear, plastic macs, 'kinky' boots and so on)?

Well, they can have treatment if they want it, but in practice very few of them do. There appear to be literally tens of thousands of men who have these particular 'kinks', as you can see by the enormous trade that is done in books and magazines devoted to pictures of women in leather aprons or plastic mackintoshes. Even the 'quality' newspapers carry quite a few discreet advertisements for firms specializing in rubber or leather clothing, and these companies are obviously doing a roaring trade.

It's generally believed that the men who have these inclinations acquired them through some sort of babyhood 'fixation' occurring at the time when they were lying gurgling happily on plastic

---

[1] *These infections—and VD—are fully dealt with in Chapter Twelve: Trouble Down Below.*

sheets or rubber mackintoshes. Fortunately, many of them are happily married to understanding wives who don't particularly mind putting on a raincoat once or twice a week to oblige their husbands.

So I think that society should leave these couples alone; they're not interfering with the rest of us and I don't see why we should make life difficult for them. Furthermore, when you look at the question dispassionately (a thing which few 'moral' crusaders ever bother to do), is there really so much difference between the 'perverted' rubber fetishist and, for example, the man who richly enjoys the feel of his expensive tweeds, or his leather gloves, or the woman who derives sensual pleasure from feeling her furs or silks next to her skin?

What about this business of bondage?

This is another difficult one. Several of the more *avant-garde* marriage manuals now quite cheerfully advocate that husbands and wives should experiment with taking turns to tie each other to the bedposts. This is all very well if you happen to enjoy fantasies of rape, (male or female), but you obviously have to be very careful what you're doing. In particular I would suggest that any couple who want to enact bondage scenes should *never* put any rope or strap around the neck area. Gags are also very unwise—it's dangerously easy for suffocation to occur.

One final point—tying your partner to the bedpost may be all very well for variety or fun with one's spouse, but for a girl to risk it with a partner she doesn't know (and trust) well could be the prelude to a tragedy : it just isn't worth the risk.

Does the same apply to things like flagellation?

Absolutely—any girl who comes across a man whose romantic overtures suddenly turn out to involve whips and knives should get her clothes on and *run* before disaster ensues.

Sadism (the infliction of pain for sexual pleasure) and its counterpart, masochism, (the acceptance of pain for similar reasons) are extraordinarily common in Britain, Northern Europe and the USA, but are probably less frequently encountered in other countries with less strict methods of childhood discipline. As we've pointed out in the chapters on love-play (*How to Handle a Woman* and *How to Handle a Man*), it's quite normal for men and women to enjoy giving and receiving *small* amounts of pain (as love bites, bottom pinching and so on). But there comes a point at which people are inflicting actual suffering on each other and obviously at this stage things are becoming pathological. If you feel that your partner's lovemaking is really getting sadistic (or, of course, masochistic) then try to get him or her to see a sympathetic doctor—before things get out of hand.

Incidentally, this also applies if the pain involved is mental rather than physical. Sadly, there are a lot of people around who obtain immense sensual gratification from being (to use a plain phrase) complete bastards to their spouses, or indeed anyone else they can manage to dominate. If a sadist, mental or physical, cannot be persuaded to seek treatment (which is usually the case), then the partner would as a rule be well advised to get out while the going's good (unless, of course, she or he happens to be a happy and contented masochist—a very rare situation).

Is it true that quite a lot of women can't help passing water at their moment of climax? Is this normal?
Yes, it's true; I wouldn't describe it as normal, but the ladies in question can't help it and the best thing is for their husbands to accept it as a bit of a joke and not to worry about it.

There's probably a slight tendency to urolagnia, as it's called, in the majority of women. We've already seen in Chapter Eight: *The Positions of Love* that there are certain intercourse postures in which the pressure of the penis on the female bladder is likely to produce (in the most normal female) a rather pleasant sensation of wanting to go to the loo.

Things go rather farther than this however, in the urolagnic woman, whose mind associates the passing of urine with intense sexual pleasure. Presumably this is due to some infantile fixation occurring during the course of early toilet training, but whatever the origin of the condition it appears to be remarkably common. An extremely popular British question-and-answer magazine (*Forum*) seems to have a vast number of urolagnic correspondents though oddly enough I don't receive all that many letters of this type myself. Most urolagnic women seem to be quite happy and don't want treatment although (for obvious reasons) they tend to have to make love in the shower or the bath, rather than in bed.

What about rectal sex?

This is a subject that people have got very upset about for centuries, not only because of the fact that they tend to associate the practice with homosexuality but (probably more important) because of the very strong conditioning most young children are given to regard their bottoms as dirty.

Rectal (anal) intercourse was for long referred to as 'the crime against nature' and in England, for instance, anybody who was found guilty of doing it was liable to the death penalty up till 1861 (though I understand that no executions were actually carried out after 1836). According to English law, this kind of 'intercourse' is still illegal between husband and wife although, oddly enough, it is accepted by law between adult consenting males.

This seems quite extraordinary, particularly as (according to a recent British Medical Association booklet) about 20% of married couples have tried the practice at some time or other. I don't know how the author got this figure but certainly there is no doubt that the practice is pretty common. After mentioning in print that it was still a crime for which husband and wife could be imprisoned, I was astonished to receive a flood of protest letters from irate couples who mostly seemed to practise anal intercourse only at period times or when the wife was suffering from some sort of vaginal problem.

The widespread belief that this practice will damage the woman's body is untrue (provided, of course, that the husband takes things *gently*). But it *does* have certain dangers: the bottom isn't exactly the cleanest part of the anatomy, and if the penis accidentally slips an inch or so forward across the skin and into the vagina (as can *very* easily happen particularly if—as is usually the case—a lubricant is used), bowel germs will be transferred from the back to the front passage. The result may be a trying vaginal discharge, or possibly a painful urinary infection. See Chapter Twelve: *Trouble Down Below*.

So, basically is anything a couple want to do OK as long as it doesn't harm their health?

Yes—as long as they *both* enjoy it. Obviously, it's a bit stupid for one of them to insist on doing something that the other one hates. We have to accept the fact that some of us are disgusted by things that other people find perfectly all right, or even great fun. Where this kind of difference of opinion happens between a husband and wife, obviously they should talk things over and try to understand each other's viewpoints.

To take a typical example, Mr. and Mrs. A very nearly came to blows over the fact that (like many men) he rather enjoyed the idea of lying and watching his wife gently stimulating her own clitoris. She regarded this suggestion as quite revolting.

Eventually, they got down to discussing the problem. She had had a repressive childhood and had been taught that masturbation was wicked (it isn't : it's normal for both males and females, even in adulthood). He had been brought up to regard women as pure, saintly creatures without sexual feelings, and he was tremendously excited by the sheer 'naughtiness' of the idea that a girl could actually want to arouse herself in this way.

So, once they'd sorted out each other's feelings and motivations they both felt a good deal better. He no longer took the attitude that he had to force her to display her sexual responsiveness, and she no longer felt that stroking her clitoris was so very sinful, though she didn't really like to try it.

Shortly afterwards, Mr. A went on a long business trip and while he was away his wife was pleased to discover that gentle self-stimulation with her finger tips was an agreeable and comforting way of relieving sexual tension. On his return, Mr. A was pleasantly surprised to find that she was quite happy to arouse his ardour now and again by draping herself senuously across the bed like some old-fashioned film vamp and stroking her vulva in a highly erotic and enticing manner!

In fact, they had both come to regard his whim not as a serious issue, but as something for them both to take pleasure in. And if there is one message that I hope this book will give, it is that humour, and joyful pleasure in bed are things of priceless importance. Laughter in lovemaking (as we said in Chapter Six) is a precious commodity, worth more than ten thousand orgasms.

FIGURE 34

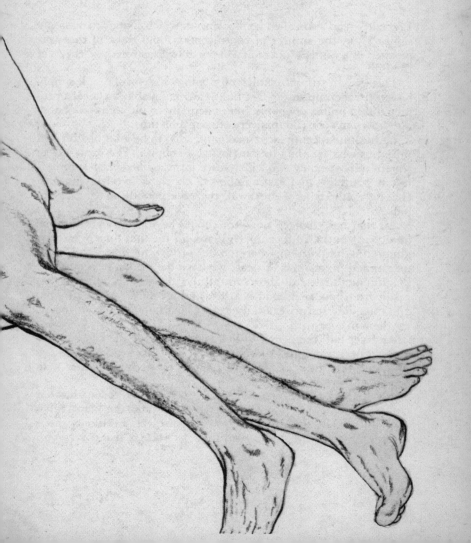

CHAPTER TEN
How to Prevent Babies

I recently read a so-called textbook of sex which contained precisely *one page,* on the subject of contraception, and most of that was devoted to a rather glum recital of possible disastrous side-effects of the Pill!

This kind of attitude is still far too common. A lot of people simply haven't woken up to the fact that really enjoyable sex means protected sex, unless of course you're actually trying to have a baby, and not many of us do that very often in a lifetime.

Until quite recently, love-making tended to be a bit of a hit and miss business for the great majority of couples. The cap and the sheath were the only two widely-used forms of medically-approved family planning, and vast numbers of people were relying on such chaotic methods as withdrawal, the 'safe period', and just plain luck.

All that has changed now—or should have. As we got into the final years of the 20th century we are, for the first time in history, almost in the position where no act of love need *ever* end in an unplanned pregnancy. At least we have the means to prevent all illegitimate births, all abortions, all the unnecessary illnesses that result from repeated child-bearing, and all the domestic troubles and tragedies that arise because people have families that are too big for them to cope with.

And yet half the people that I talk to haven't the foggiest idea about contraception! Abortion rates are still soaring, and it's probable that most babies still happen by accident rather than design.

It's high time we put all this right, firstly by educating our children about the need for contraception (and the help that is available), and secondly by educating ourselves. Everyone who is having sex or who might have sex (and, let's face it, that covers most of the adult and teenage population) owes it to himself or herself to find out about the various techniques of birth control and to use them—every time.

This chapter tells you about all the methods that are currently available (new ones may be along soon) so that you can make up your mind which one will best suit you and your partner.

After tens of thousands of years of human existence, reliable family planning is here at last. Let's make sure we use it!

The Pill

The ordinary type of oral contraceptive pill provides very nearly 100% reliability in preventing unwanted pregnancies. It's true that a doctor will very occasionally come across women who say that they've got pregnant while on it, but it's probable that what's really happened is that they have forgotten to take their nightly Pill—since a little investigation usually shows that these are patients who are not very good at getting themselves organized to take tablets, or to keep records of their periods. If that applies to you, then perhaps you'd better look for some other form of contraception.

At the time of writing there about 25 different brands of Pill on the market, and new ones are constantly being introduced. Indeed, the advance of research in this field is so fast that almost anything one writes about the Pill is bound to become outdated quite soon. There is a newer kind of contraceptive called the Mini-Pill, but most of this section will be devoted to the 'ordinary' or 'combined' Pill—which is by far the most widely used.

The ordinary type of Pill is called 'combined' because it contains a combination of two different hormones. These vary from brand to brand, but one is always an *oestrogen* and the other a *progestogen*. By switching a patient from one brand to another, the doctor is

July	1	2	3	4	5	6	7	8	9	10	11	12	13	14	15	16	17	18
period				////	////	////	////	////										
tablets								T	T	T	T	T	T	T	T	T	T	T
remarks													S					S
period	////	////																
tablets				T	T	T	T	T	T	T	T	T	T	T	T	T	T	T
remarks																		
August																		

usually able to control any minor side-effects which may occur (see below).

The principles of Pill-taking are quite simple. Each pack contains 21 Pills (22 in the case of one brand), which means that you take one every night for three weeks, and then have a week's break. During that week, you will normally have a period. It's the 'cut-off' of hormones when you finish your packet of Pills that brings menstruation on. You can see what I mean from the illustration (figure 38), which shows a typical 'Pill-chart'. Life will be a lot easier for you and your doctor if you can arrange to fill in one of these records for your first few months on the Pill.

In this case, the patient who has decided to take an oral contraceptive is a girl whose period normally lasts for about seven days. Note that she has shaded in the days of menstruation, starting on July 4th.

In her particular case, her doctor has told her to count the first day of her period as Day One and to start taking the Pill on Day Five. She takes the oral contraceptive every night for 21 days (filling in a T for 'tablet taken' as a reminder each time) and, a couple of days after finishing this first packet, her period comes on again.

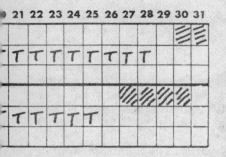

21 22 23 24 25 26 27 28 29 30 31

FIGURE 38

▨	menstruation
T	tablet taken
S	spotting

Notice that it only lasts for four days this time. Most women find to their pleasure that on the Pill menstruation is a good deal less heavy, shorter and *much* less painful than previously. Note also that the woman won't be protected till she's been on the Pill for two weeks.

You can see that, after seven days off, the girl starts on her *second* pack of tablets and thenceforward she takes the Pill 'three weeks on and one week off.'

An alternative – and newer – way of starting the Pill is to 'kick off' on Day One of that first period. If you do this, you *needn't* take any extra precautions; you'll be protected right away.

SIDE-EFFECTS. The severity and incidence of side-effects of the Pill have been greatly exaggerated in the past. It's important to stress that the majority of women have *no* problems at all on the Pill, and a lot of people feel far better than they did before, not just because of the beneficial effect on menstruation that we've already mentioned, but because of the sheer bliss of being free of the risk of unwanted pregnancy.

However it is true that many women do get very minor problems, most of which vanish after a few months. If they don't, a carefully-planned change of brand will usually do the trick.

One of the commonest side-effects is spotting of blood occurring between periods (and sometimes requiring the use of a pad or tampon). You can see that the girl in our illustration (figure 38) had this problem, but that the spotting (marked as 'S' on her Pill-chart) vanished after the first month.

Nausea, slight weight increase (particularly in the breasts) and tiredness are also quite frequently encountered. It's probable that some women are genuinely made depressed by the Pill, but depression is so common these days that one has to be wary of attributing it to the use of an oral contraceptive, especially as some patients—and doctors—have a tendency to blame anything from athlete's foot to walking in front of a bus on the poor old Pill! It's well-known that if you put a group of people on a completely inert 'placebo' tablet *and tell them it's the Pill*, quite a proportion of them will develop all sorts of side effects, and even have to stop taking the tablets.

Argument continues about whether the oral contraceptive causes decreased sexual desire. Frankly, I'm not very convinced that it really does. Many women say their enthusiasm for love-making is increased but this may simply reflect their new-found confidence that they are not going to get pregnant.

Similarly, a woman who says that the Pill has diminished her desire may only be interested in love-making when there is a spice of danger, and she may find sex dull if there is absolutely no chance of pregnancy. Alternatively, she may be one of a quite substantial minority of women who find seminal fluid disgusting, which is why all is well when the husband uses a sheath, but why trouble arises when the couple switch to the Pill.

Last among the minor side-effects, I would mention that the Pill does make you rather more vulnerable to the common vaginal infection called thrush (see Chapter Twelve: *Trouble Down Below*). Thrush is easily treated, however, and it's pretty rare for anyone to have to come off the Pill because of it.

There are a few other possible side-effects (for example, absence of periods), but your doctor will discuss these with you if necessary. Incidentally, so far as we can tell at the present time, the Pill does not appear to carry a risk of causing cancer of the womb, breast or any other organ. At the moment, there is some evidence that it actually protects a woman against certain breast troubles.

The one really serious side-effect that woman always worry about—and quite rightly so—is the question of thrombosis (clotting—usually in the veins of the legs).

There's no doubt that (contrary to the claims of some of the manufacturers back in the early 1960s) this danger really does exist. Women on the Pill do die of thrombosis every year, but fortunately the risk of such tragedies is very remote indeed, unless you are a heavy smoker or have some other risk factor. And the risk of dying because of pregnancy is far, far greater than that of death from the oral contraceptive.

So, a great number of women (including a lot of doctors, doctors' wives and nurses) feel that, for them, the benefits of the Pill far outweigh the remote risk of thrombosis. Happily, deaths from this cause have fallen very markedly since the oestrogen content of all widely-prescribed Pills was lowered to 50 microgrammes or less back in 1969. Up till that time, many Pills had contained 100 microgrammes of oestrogen.

How can you try to prevent serious side-effects occurring? Simply by going to a Family Planning Clinic or General Practitioner's surgery where you will have a proper clinical history taken *before* you start on the Pill. The doctor will tell you if he feels this kind of contraceptive would not suit you. But if he thinks that (as is the case with most women) the Pill will be quite OK for you, he'll want to see you again and to keep a careful check on your progress. Many doctors working in the field of family planning see their patients six weeks after starting the Pill, then every three months or so for the first year and six monthly thereafter, with more frequent visits if necessary.

This is in sharp contrast to the practice in certain areas of the world, where the Pill is sold over shop counters. Admittedly, oral contraceptives have been in use since about 1956 (when the first tests were being conducted in Puerto Rico), but the time has certainly not come for them to be dished out like wholesale groceries. I would frankly not advise a woman to go to a doctor anywhere in the world who issues Pill prescriptions without seeing the patient.

RISK FACTORS The massive amount of research done in the past 10 years indicates that the Pill is very, very safe for women who do not have certain 'risk factors'. These risk factors include (a) being a heavy smoker; (b) being over 35; (c) having a serious family history of heart attacks and thrombosis. Also at some additional risk are people who have high blood pressure, people who are very overweight, and people with diabetes.

THE 'MINI-PILL'. This is a catchy but rather misleading name for Pills which contain progestogens only, and no oestrogen at all. As we've already mentioned, oestrogens are thought to be mainly (not entirely) responsible for the occurrence of thrombosis, so the mini-Pill ought to be even safer than the low oestrogen Pill.

Unfortunately, these Pills are associated with some risk of pregnancy. It's probable that if 100 women took the mini-Pill for a year, between two and three of them might become pregnant. This kind of preparation is mainly used by the over-35s and by women who are breast-feeding (since it doesn't stop the milk).

The mini-Pill is taken *continuously*, that is every night without a break, and this means that menstrual cycle control is not so good as with the ordinary Pill, since irregular bleeding does tend to occur. If your period comes early or late, *don't* stop taking the mini-Pill. Continue to take one every night whether you are menstruating or not.

The IUD or IUCD (the Loop or Coil)

The Intra-Uterine Device (or Intra-Uterine Contraceptive Device) is probably the second best 'baby-preventer' after the Pill. If 100 women use it for a year, only about two of them will become pregnant. However, nearly 100% safety can be achieved by using a chemical contraceptive in addition, so the woman with an IUD can feel pretty well protected if she just slips a pessary (see below) into her vagina five minutes before love-making.

What exactly is an IUD? It's just a small object that is inserted into the womb (the uterus) in order to prevent pregnancy. The commonest type is called the loop or coil—you can see why by looking at figure 39, which shows a loop in place inside the womb.

The loop is made of plastic, and is only about two inches from top to bottom, but that's quite big enough for it to fill the cavity of the womb. The plastic is flexible, and the loop is supplied straightened out (in a sterile tube), so that the doctor can easily pass it through the vagina and slip it through the neck of the womb—a procedure which normally takes only a minute or so. Once inside, the loop takes up its natural shape again.

You'll see from the picture that there are two little threads dangling down into the vagina. These have two functions. Firstly, the doctor (or you) can feel these threads from time to time and so ensure that the IUD is in place (he'll probably want to see you every six or 12 months to check this). Secondly, if the loop has to be removed, all the doctor has to do is to grasp the threads firmly with an instrument and tug.

Are there any disadvantages to the loop? Well, everything medical has its side-effects and the IUD is no exception. About 85% of women who have them fitted get along very well after the first few months, but a minority of women do have to have the devices removed, mainly because of heavy periods or period pain.

In general, doctors are not very keen on fitting IUDs into women who already have very heavy periods or a lot of period pain. These symptoms are relieved by the Pill, which is therefore usually a better choice of contraceptive for these patients.

Uncommon complications of the IUD include pelvic infection

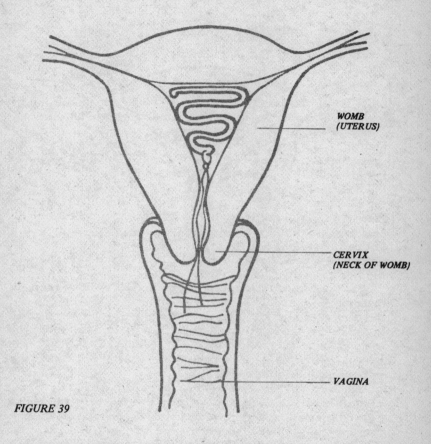

**WOMB
(UTERUS)**

**CERVIX
(NECK OF WOMB)**

VAGINA

FIGURE 39

and the occurrence of pregnancy in an abnormal site (ectopic pregnancy), which is very rare.

Most women seem to have heard of loops going into the wrong place. It's quite true that they are sometimes pushed into the wall of the womb at insertion, but they are never 'lost', as people often

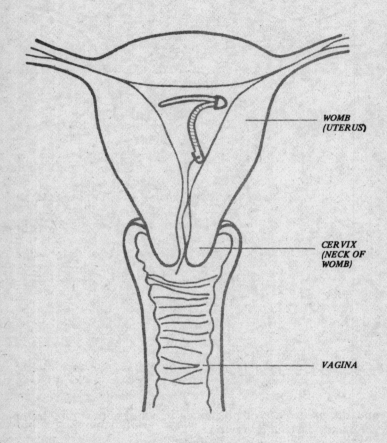

WOMB
(UTERUS)

CERVIX
(NECK OF
WOMB)

VAGINA

FIGURE 40

imagine.

The other story patients have heard is that it's possible for coils to fall out, and for pregnancy to occur as a result. As a male, I find it very hard to imagine how anybody can fail to notice something the size of an IUD tumbling out, but undoubtedly this does happen from time to time. Furthermore, it is possible for a loop to slip down into the vagina without actually falling out onto the floor, and for this not to be noticed at intercourse. This is really all the more reason why a lady with a loop should practise checking the threads herself, say once a week or so.

At present very few family doctors are equipped to insert loops, so if you are interested in the idea you will probably have to go to a Family Planning Clinic or to a gynecologist. Normally an IUD is inserted just after a period, but a very good time to have one fitted is immediately after childbirth (or a termination or miscarriage). Your obstetrician may well be willing to do this for you, but *don't* tell him what you want the day before you leave hospital; make your intentions clear in plenty of time.

NEWER TYPES OF IUD. The loop and other older types of IUD aren't normally prescribed for a girl who hasn't yet had a pregnancy (because the passage through the neck of the womb will be pretty narrow).

But in the early 1970s, several new types of IUD were introduced which can be inserted without difficulty even if a woman has never been pregnant. Chief among these are the Dalkon shield and the Copper Seven (Cu-7, or Gravigard).

The Copper Seven (which you can see in figure 40) has proved the most popular of these devices so far. It is formed from a piece of plastic in the shape of a figure 7, and round the stem of the 7 is wrapped a very fine copper wire. A tiny amount of copper seeps out of the device every day and for this reason it is at present recommended that the Copper Seven is replaced by another one every two years or so, before the old one is worn out. Removal is usually very easy, since all the doctor has to do is to tug on the thread, as with other types of IUD. The new IUDs now seem to be preferable to the old ones, since they have a lower pregnancy rate and are less likely to be expelled or to cause side-effects. They will probably become much more commonly used than the 'traditional' loop or coil before very long.

The Sheath and Pessary

I mention the sheath and the pessary together *since the first should not be used without the second*. The sheath (condom, French letter or Durex) is a thin rubber device that slips over the penis. The pessary is a vaginal tablet that kills sperms. Incidentally, no-one need feel guilty about killing sperms: any number up to 500 million die during any one act of intercourse.

Why should a pessary be used with a sheath? For the very good reason that even the best condoms (contrary to the manufacturers' claims) do break or leak at times. If this happens, the pessary will probably be able to cope with any sperms that get through.

The sheath remains the most widely-used form of birth control in many countries, and will probably continue its popularity for many years to come. Used with the pessary, it's really a pretty good method of family planning, though not as safe as the Pill or the IUD. If you want to use it, you'd do well to remember the following points.

(1) always buy a reputable brand of sheath (in Britain, the packet should carry the BSI Kite mark)—*not* some cut-price brand on a market stall.

(2) Similarly, always get a good brand of pessary, preferably one prescribed by your doctor or Family Planning Clinic. Some years ago, the Consumer Association of Great Britain showed by a series of careful tests that many over-the-counter brands of pessary were practically useless.

(3) Insert the pessary into the highest part of the vagina five minutes before intercourse (as shown in figure 41) to give it time to dissolve. If you continue making love for more than an hour, use another pessary.

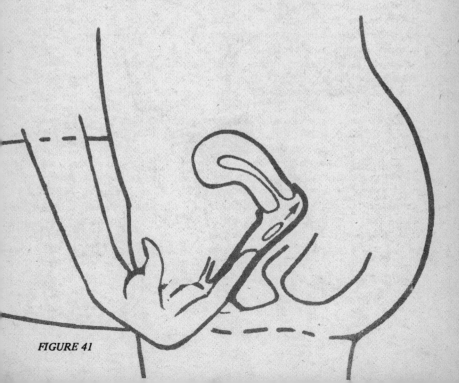

FIGURE 41

(4) Put the sheath on carefully (see figure 42) *before intercourse begins.* For heaven's sake don't make the common (and potentially disastrous) mistake of donning it half way through, because the tiny drops of fluid that come from a man's penis long before he reaches his climax may well contain sperms.

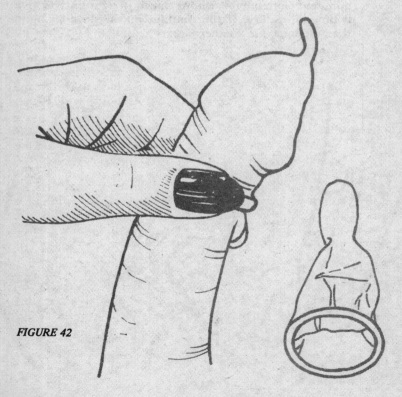

FIGURE 42

Some people do feel that for the man to put on the sheath in the middle of love play is rather cold and clinical. The answer to this is quite simple—the woman can put it on for him, as in figure 42. In Scandinavia this is recognized as quite an important and exciting part of love play.

(5) Be careful that you don't spill any fluid when you withdraw from the vagina after the climax. The 'short' sheathes, which only fit over the head of the penis are very dangerous from this point of view and I certainly wouldn't recommend them.

Drawbacks of the Sheath and Pessary method. These are very few. Occasionally people develop sensitivity reactions to the condom, to the lubricant on it, or (more commonly) to the pessary. In the latter case, a change to a different brand of pessary is all that is required.

Quite often, a wife says that her husband 'can't get on with' the sheath. This often implies that the unfortunate man is suffering from impotence, which is fully discussed in Chapter Eleven: *Problems with Sex.*

Really, the only major problem with this method is that for many couples it doesn't *feel* as good as making love without a sheath. If using the very finest and thinnest condoms (which are also the most expensive) doesn't help, then it's really best to switch to some other technique of contraception.

The Cap

In the pre-Pill and pre-IUD days, caps were very widely prescribed indeed, but this is no longer so today. However, this remains a very useful and fairly safe method of family planning, about as effective as the sheath and pessary technique, but not as safe as the Pill or IUD.

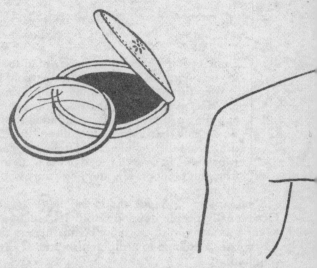

FIGURE 43

The cap is simply a rubber or plastic device that the wife pops into the vagina to form a physical barrier that will keep the sperms from getting to the neck of the womb. It *must* be used with a chemical agent (a spermicidal cream or gel) that is smeared on it just before insertion.

There are quite a number of different types of cap, including the cervical cap or Dutch cap, the vault cap, the vimule and the Prencap. I don't have space to discuss them all here,[1] so we'll just deal with what is still by far the most commonly used type—the diaphragm.

You can see what the diaphragm looks like in figure 43. It isn't the most beautiful thing in the world, but then it isn't meant to be admired! However, as you can see, diaphragms do come in rather nice-looking cases—like powder compacts—which can readily be slipped into the handbag.

[1] *They will, however, be dealt with fully in a forthcoming book* Carefree Love, *the Home Doctor Book of Contraception.*

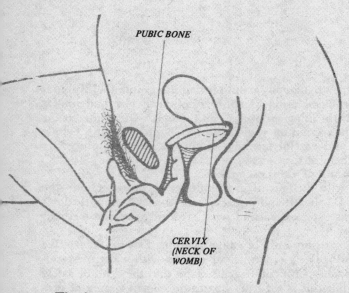

The insertion of a diaphragm requires careful teaching by a doctor or nurse. You can see in the picture that the idea is to get it to lie (normally dome upwards) so that it's tucked up behind the ledge of the pubic bone, with the other edge behind the cervix, or neck of the womb. You should be able to feel the cervix through it when it's in position.

Disadvantages of the Cap. These are few, though occasional cases of sensitivity to rubber or to the spermicide do occur. Many women complain that the device interferes with the spontaneity of love-making, and it's quite true that on a cold winter's night nothing could be less romantic than for the poor wife to have to get out of bed and start trying to insert her cap! The answer is, of course, that a woman who makes love regularly can insert her cap *every evening* before going to bed, leaving it in till the following morning. In short, the best place for the cap is in the vagina.

Women who are nervous about putting things into their vaginas may have problems using a cap. Very often they've had similar difficulties with using tampons, and indeed with intercourse itself. (See the section on vaginismus in Chapter Eleven). Gentle reassurance and careful teaching of correct insertion procedure will usually help in these cases.

Other Methods of Contraception

We've dealt with the four main techniques of contraception—the Pill, the IUD, sheath-and-pessary, and the cap—and I don't propose to waste space discussing what are frankly inferior methods in great detail.

Chemical barriers are only of value when used in the way we've already described (e.g. spermicidal creams with a cap). Manufacturers of some spermicidal agents claim that they can be safely used alone, but this is *not* true. Foams do offer a degree of protection, but some husbands feel as if they are fighting a fire rather than making love. C-films are less messy and moderately effective.

The rhythm method is very unreliable for the reasons already explained in Chapter Three: *How Sex Leads to Babies*. If you feel that because of religious principles you definitely should use this method, then it is best that you contact the Catholic Marriage Advisory Service who will tell you how to try to work out a 'safe period' with the aid of a temperature chart like that described in the section on infertility in Chapter Thirteen.

Withdrawal (*coitus interruptus*) is not only frustrating but a very good way of getting pregnant. Of 100 fertile wives whose husbands practise withdrawal, it's probable that about 18 will be pregnant at the end of a year. The frightening thing is that so many people (usually those who can least afford to get pregnant) still use this crazy and most unreliable method of contraception.

Certain other hopeless or frankly mythical methods of contraception are discussed briefly in Chapter Three: *How Sex Leads to Babies*.

Sterilization

Note: any surgical operation can occasionally go wrong, and anyone contemplating sterilization should discuss possible adverse effects with their doctor.

Female Sterilization is carried out by a fairly straightforward operation under general anaesthetic which involves opening the abdomen and cutting through the two Fallopian tubes. As you can see from figure 44 this means that sperms can no longer reach the eggs, which, when released by the ovaries, now disappear harmlessly inside the abdomen.

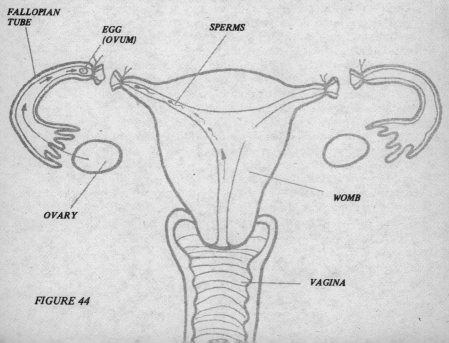

FALLOPIAN TUBE

EGG (OVUM)

SPERMS

OVARY

WOMB

VAGINA

FIGURE 44

The operation is effective right away in preventing pregnancy. It should be regarded as irreversible when it is undertaken, though in *exceptional* circumstances a gynaecologist may be willing to attempt to rejoin the tubes.

Laparoscopic sterilization is a technique in which the surgeon doesn't need to cut open the abdominal wall. Instead, he performs the operation with a sort of surgical telescope, which is pushed through a relatively small hole in the tummy. This means that the woman has a much quicker recovery and a shorter time in hospital.

N.B. Laparoscopic sterilization is, however, much more technically difficult to perform than ordinary sterilisation. Complications are not infrequent except in the most skilled hands.

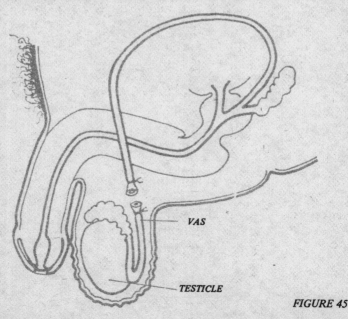

VAS

TESTICLE

FIGURE 45

Male sterilization (*vasectomy*) is now becoming a very popular operation indeed. It's a lot simpler than female sterilization, and is normally done under a local anaesthetic. You can see what happens in figure 45—the surgeon simply cuts through the tube (the vas) that carries sperms upwards from the testicles to the penis. From looking at figure 46, you can see that only a tiny nick on each side is required.

Recovery from the operation is pretty rapid, and many men need take only one day off work. The procedure doesn't affect the patient's virility in any way (unless, of course, he has deep psychological problems which lead him to feel he has been castrated) and he will continue to produce seminal fluid at orgasm.

It's very important to stress that the effect of vasectomy is *not*

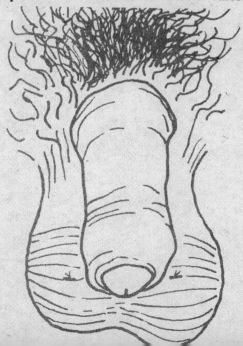

FIGURE 46

immediate. There will probably be sperms in the fluid for several months after the operation, so some form of contraception must be used until the husband is given the 'all clear' by the surgeon, usually after two specimens of seminal fluid have been checked by the lab.

Like female sterilization, vasectomy is best regarded as irreversible at the time of operation, but a surgeon may sometimes be willing to try to rejoin the cut ends of the vas, for instance if a man's family have been wiped out in an accident. In the USA, 'sperm banks', where a man 'makes a deposit' before the operation, are coming into use but it's not yet clear how valuable or effective these will be.

Abortion is not to be regarded as a method of family planning, but rather as a failure of contraception. It is dealt with fully in Chapter Fourteen. The 'morning-after' pill and menstrual extraction are also dealt with in Chapter Fourteen.

CHAPTER ELEVEN
Problems with Sex

The vast majority of sexual problems are psychological and not physical.

This statement comes as a great surprise to most people. The man who is impotent and the woman whose vagina is 'too small' or 'too tender' for pain-free intercourse naturally assume that there is some *physical* cause ('a blockage of blood flow', or 'a thick hymen') but this is very rarely so. There are many exceptions, of course, (see Chapter Twelve : *Trouble Down Below*), which is why anybody with this kind of difficulty needs a proper physical examination. But, generally, a person whose sex life isn't going too well has problems located in the mind—*not* in the sex organs.

In fact, a large part of the treatment of these illnesses is to try to get the affected husband or wife to accept that the trouble is psychological rather than physical. This can be very hard indeed, especially as the patient may well have acquired the most extraordinary notions about the cause of the difficulty from friends or from old fashioned medical books. For example, in almost every public library in Britain, there is a medical dictionary which cheerfully informs the sufferer from impotence that his problem may be due to syphilis of the spinal cord, various unpleasant glandular disorders, 'abnormality of sexual desire', or—on a more mundane level—'a tight foreskin'. I may say that though such things are possible I have *never* seen a man whose impotence was due to any of these conditions.

The next thing to realize is that husbands and wives with sexual problems usually have to be treated *together*. Except in rare cases, there isn't a lot of point in advising one partner and not the other. So often it's not just the husband (or just the wife) who needs help, it's the marriage. So the 'marital unit' (to use the currently fashionable phrase) must be given therapy as a whole.

A lot of people find this very hard to understand, but the man whose wife can't relax her vagina to let him in must realize that if *he* were to learn more about the technique of love play (see Chapter Six: *How to Handle a Woman*), *she* would find it very much easier to become less tense. Similarly, the woman whose husband is a premature ejaculator has to be taught methods of love making that will help him overcome this trouble.

Furthermore, it's a fairly basic rule in sexual medicine that if one partner has a problem, the other very often has one too. Indeed it's quite fantastic how frequently the woman with frigidity or vaginismus marries a man who is impotent.

Sometimes the 'healthy' partner will indignantly deny that he or she has any difficulty at all, in the face of overwhelming evidence to the contrary! I once saw a man who had become impotent immediately after his wedding and who eventually revealed the fact that his middle-aged wife had been through not one but two marriages and was still a virgin. She had a very severe case of vaginismus (being quite terrified of anything being put into her vagina), so it was no wonder that her approach to love making administered the *coup de grâce* to her husband's somewhat shaky potency. Yet she found it more or less impossible to understand that *she* needed treatment too, as she considered that it was her husband who was the patient and not her.

No Magic Remedies

I want to make clear that because these problems arise in the emotions, there are absolutely no magic remedies for them. People are 'programmed' in early life where sexual matters are concerned and if they have been given the impression that sex is dirty, or frightening, or violent, then there is every likelihood that they are then going to have marital difficulties when they grow up. Similarly, any child who has not been able to develop a warm, loving, fear-free relationship with his or her parents is very likely to run into immense sexual problems in adulthood. Obviously to get rid of these repressions, conflicts and anxieties is a prolonged and difficult business, and the doctor or therapist will have to have quite a number of long discussions with both husband and wife, probably over a period of months.

It's perfectly natural for people to want a magic pill or a wonderful operation that will put everything right; but life just isn't like that. Occasionally one comes across patients who say that their sexual troubles have been corrected by some aphrodisiac (love potion) or sex aid bought in a shop. That's fine for them, but I think the rest of us should realize that this is a 'placebo effect' —in other words, they got better because they *believed* that whatever it was that they spent their money on would cure them.

For most people, however, eliminating any kind of serious sexual problem is likely to be a slow business, even in the care of a skilled therapist. At present the most effective therapy for sexual difficulties is that carried out at the American Reproductive Biology Research Foundation in St. Louis under the direction of Masters and Johnson. This involves a period of residential treatment for both husband and wife under the care of two highly skilled psychotherapists, who go very fully into the emotional background of both partners.

Naturally, this kind of intensive therapy is expensive (particularly for those who have to pay their air fares to the USA) and for this reason it is never going to be universally available to everyone with a marriage problem. But happily, the St. Louis team's researches have so revolutionized the treatment of sexual difficulties that many doctors and marriage guidance counsellors all over the world are finding that they can get quite good results with modifications of Masters and Johnson's methods, and without the need for the husband and wife to have 'in-patient' care. However, these results are *not* obtained overnight—they're only likely to be achieved where the husband and wife are willing to cooperate with the therapist (and with each other) over a period of many weeks or months in unravelling the tensions that have caused their difficulty.

How common are marriage problems?

In the USA it's estimated that sexual troubles affect about 50% of all marriages at some time or other. A recent study in Britain showed that the staggering figure of 57% of 25 year old adults admitted some sort of sexual difficulty but that only 2% had consulted a doctor. Happily, sexual problems seem to be becoming slightly less common these days, reflecting the fact that the upbringing of children isn't quite as repressive as it once was. However any doctor working in the field of family planning will confirm that day after day, week after week, in come a long succession of bewildered couples with various sexual hang-ups, chiefly vaginismus and frigidity in woman, and impotence and premature ejaculation in men (all these conditions are dealt with later in this chapter). In short, sex problems are a good deal commoner than measles—and cause far, far more trouble.

Now the great American experts in sexual medicine, Masters and Johnson, have rightly condemned the 'cookbook' approach to sexual difficulties. I quite agree that few people with a really serious psychosexual problem are likely to be helped just by reading a book. However couples who have *mild* difficulties in bed can certainly gain some benefit from being given helpful literature to read. So the object of this chapter is to try to help these men and women, and also to give more severely affected couples some idea of what kind of professional assistance is now available. There's no doubt that somebody with a really deep seated psychosexual problem does need the help of a trained therapist (a doctor, a psychologist or a marriage guidance counsellor), and shouldn't try to blunder on alone.

Until quite recently, such help was almost impossible to obtain (except if you happened to be both rich and determined) but the last few years have seen something of a revolution in sexual therapy, and more and more general practitioners, psychiatrists, gynecologists and family planning specialists are taking an interest in this field. In Britain, America and most Western countries the position now is that you *can* get help and advice at a modest cost provided that you really want it and are willing to keep on searching until you find it.

In fact however, a lot of people with sexual problems *don't* really want to get better, perhaps because deep down they're happy as they are. It is obvious from their approach to the doctor that they would like either to be told that nothing can be done, or else that they should break the marriage and seek a new partner. If you genuinely want to sort out your marital problem, read this chapter and then go and talk to your own doctor, or the doctor at your nearest Family Planning Clinic, or a Marriage Guidance Counsellor. If they can't help, ask them to send you to someone who will, and do persist until you feel you are getting the help that's right for you.

Female Psychosexual Problems

The wife who has sexual difficulties has almost invariably had a repressive childhood. She has either been told very little about sex (and therefore got the idea that it was an unmentionable subject), or else learned to associate it with ideas of painful childbirth, vaginal bleeding, violence, rape and so on. Indeed, a small but probably significant proportion of these unfortunate wives give a history of having themselves been raped, or nearly raped, in early life.

It is tragic that a girl's normal healthy sexuality should be maimed in this way, and any society that does this to a happy uncomplicated child has a lot to answer for. It's not fair to blame the affected woman's parents or teachers, for after all they themselves were merely the victims of the repressions of their own childhood. We can only hope that with the advent of a less inhibited and less sexually hung-up society, women will one day be freed from these psychological shackles that have been placed upon them.

There are two main types of female psychosexual dysfunction—*vaginismus* and *frigidity*.

VAGINISMUS. This is a big word, but all it means is that whenever a sexual approach is made to the affected woman, the muscles round the opening of her vagina close down like a mouth saying 'No!' She doesn't mean this to happen, but she can't help it. Indeed, she probably doesn't know it's occurring at all. To her, it seems as though her vagina is tremendously narrow, or painful, or as if there's some obstruction (like the hymen, or virgin's veil which is described in Chapter Two) preventing the penis from getting in. Of course, there isn't a physical barrier and the whole problem is caused by muscular spasm. This is aggravated by dryness of the vagina, because only when a woman is both relaxed and sexually excited will the love juices flow. (For techniques of making them flow, see Chapter Six: *How to*

Handle a Woman.)

Let's look at a typical case history. Sarah had grown up without being told much about sex, except for her mother's and her aunts' occasional references to the dreadful pain of childbirth ('you'll suffer like me too, dear'), plus a few dark hints about the indignities a wife has to put up with at her husband's hands.

The result was practically inevitable. Sarah was secretly terrified of her own vagina. She thought of it as a tight, narrow passage up which one day some rapist of a husband would force his sharp and agonizing penis.

When puberty came, she was very frightened by the unexpected onset of menstruation. This alarming and painful phenomenon reinforced her worst fears about her vagina. Other girls at school suggested that she use tampons, but she was horrified by the whole idea, and her few attempts to insert them were disastrous, with poor Sarah ending up in tears. Incidentally, a history of never being able to insert a Tampax is so absolutely typical of vaginismus that I call it 'the Tampax test'.

Sarah's few boy friends never got very far with her, because she practically doubled up every time one of them tried to touch her anywhere between the shoulders and the knees. Eventually she met James, a quiet and very religious boy with whom she got along very well indeed. He made few overtures before marriage and she agreed with her mother who expressed the opinion that 'he wouldn't trouble her very often'.

But underneath his quiet exterior and reserve, James was a fairly lusty young man who had every intention of enjoying his wedding night to the full. Unfortunately, he was completely unskilled in bed and his rather rough overtures stood no chance at all where Sarah was concerned. In short, the honeymoon was a fiasco, and Sarah spent half the time in tears.

Happily, James didn't respond in the way that many husbands in this kind of situation do—by becoming impotent. Instead, he very sensibly insisted that Sarah went to her local Family Planning Clinic. Even though the doctor there was a woman, it was some time before Sarah would let herself be examined.

But at last the doctor managed to persuade her to relax enough for a gloved finger to be inserted into her vagina. Once this was done, it was as if Sarah's citadel had been stormed at last. The understanding doctor was able to sit (still with one finger in Sarah's vagina) and talk to her about her deepest fears. And as Sarah talked, her vaginal muscles at last began to relax.

The doctor then got her to pop her own finger into the vagina. Like most girls in this situation, she was pleasurably surprised at how roomy and wide her love passage was. After several weeks of reassurance from the doctor (and daily self-exploration of her vagina), she was eventually able to let her husband slip a finger inside her. For his part, of course, he had to be taught how to arouse her in order to make her vaginal muscles relax and her love juices flow.

It was several months later before she had unwound enough to allow actual intercourse, but from then on things improved rapidly and eventually the two of them were able to enjoy a happy and normal sex life.

Many cases of vaginismus are nowhere near as bad as that, but others (particularly those that have been established for some years) are much worse. The great thing is <u>not to let the condition go on,</u> because the best chance of cure is to seek skilled help as early as possible.

FRIGIDITY. I dislike this word, which has a rather sneering sort of sound about it, but the strictly medical terms like 'orgasmic impairment' or 'primary and secondary situational orgasmic dysfunction' are such mouthfuls that it seems better to stick to the popular expression.

So, let me just explain that by 'frigidity' I mean lack of sexual desire and, more specifically, inability to reach a climax. When I say that a woman is frigid, I *don't* mean that she is emotionally cold and withdrawn for she may perfectly well be a warm and loving person who is desperately struggling to express her sexuality.

Let me also make it absolutely clear that a woman who is frigid does *not* have a problem with her clitoris or vagina. Any number of wives who can't reach a climax think it must be because they don't have the right nerve connections round the love passage, or that the clitoris is 'too high' or 'hidden'. This is all nonsense—and I must repeat that frigidity occurs in the mind, *not* in the lower abdomen.

What can be done about the problem then? Let's look at a case history of a woman who was successful in overcoming her inhibitions and so losing her frigidity.

Margaret was 35 and had been married for 12 years. Her problem distressed her to such an extent that even when trying to explain what was wrong with her, she burst into tears.

'It's dreadful,' she sobbed, 'I try desperately hard, but whenever I think I'm about to come, my husband reaches his climax and that's that.'

For a start, Margaret was *trying too hard*. Like an impotent male, she was so tensed up about her performance before she started that there wasn't the remotest chance of success. Her doctor listened to her fears, spent some time in reassuring her

FIGURE 35

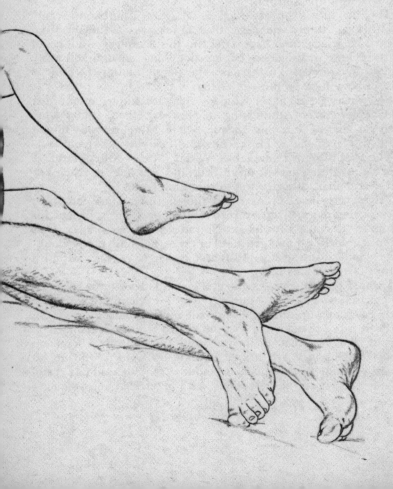

that she was physically quite normal, and then prescribed a mild tranquillizer at bedtime to help her relax. (Some patients prefer a sherry or a dry Martini.)

Then he turned his attention to Margaret's husband, Frank. Before long, it became clear that Frank was a sufferer from premature ejaculation (see later in this chapter) who could scarcely have maintained his erection long enough to satisfy almost any woman. Furthermore, he simply hadn't the faintest idea of how to caress his wife's body.

So Frank was taught the basic love play techniques, as outlined in Chapter Six, of stimulating the breasts, clitoris and vagina with his fingers, lips and tongue, while Margaret was taught methods of prolonging his erection and delaying his climax.

The results were remarkable. Within a few weeks Margaret became much less tensed up in bed, and was able to reach her first ever climax, as a result of tongue stimulation.

Before very long, Frank could prolong intercourse for up to 15 or 20 minutes, which turned out to be quite sufficient for Margaret to reach her climax. Nowadays, on the odd occasions when she doesn't quite 'get there in time', her husband is almost always able to bring her to orgasm by finger caresses within a matter of 10 seconds or so.

I would guess that throughout the world there must be many millions of women like Margaret who are victims, not just of their own hang-ups, but of sheer male incompetence.

There are, of course, many other wives who remain frigid despite the fact that their husbands are perfectly competent lovers. Often, they are strictly brought-up women who are so afraid of losing control of their emotions that they simply *cannot* let themselves go in bed. 'It seems as if I'm terrified to let the fuses blow', as one wife put it.

These patients can often be helped by discussion of their anxieties. Interestingly, they may start to get better as soon as they have the doctor's assurance that it's quite all right for a respectable married woman to have a climax! This frequently happens when the doctor is also a female, and it's quite obvious that the patient is seeing her as a substitute for her own mother, since up until then the assumption has been that 'Mother wouldn't like it . . . ' Once again, however, treatment is likely to be a prolonged, but very worthwhile business.

Quite a lot of women with vaginismus or frigidity can be helped by the technique known as 'desensitization therapy', which is described under the heading IMPOTENCE. Others may sometimes be helped by the use of a vibrator (see Chapter Nine). They may find the sensation it produces quite comforting and, (since they have the device under their own control) it is not as frightening for them as a penis might be. A vibrator is certainly worth trying in the case of a frigid woman who for some reason is currently without a partner.

Male Psychosexual Problems

Any male who has started reading here had better go back to the beginning of the chapter and begin again, for it's important that he should realize that male as well as female sexual problems are almost invariably psychological in origin and the man who has troubles in bed usually has problems stretching way back to babyhood.

He may perhaps have come from a strictly religious family in which sex was never mentioned. (Without wishing to offend anybody's religious principles, I should mention that it is no secret that male—and female—sexual hang-ups are much commoner among people with a very strict Catholic, Presbyterian or Orthodox Jewish background.) He may have had an authoritarian father who imposed impossible standards of conduct on him, or he may have had a mother who was obsessed with ideas of 'hygiene' and who taught him that his sex organs were 'dirty'.

Much of this early conditioning he will have forgotten, but it will have stayed in his subconscious all his life. So, he will probably have had a good deal of guilt about the entirely healthy and normal teenage practice of masturbation—and when it comes to intercourse itself he will be teetering on the brink of disaster, because deep down a little anxiety-provoking voice is saying: 'What you're doing is WRONG!'

So, it is anxiety that underlies male sexual problems. And only treatment directed to alleviating that anxiety will be of any value.

IMPOTENCE. Impotence means partial or complete inability to get an erection. I mention this because people so often misunderstand the word, frequently confusing it with *infertility*. (See Chapter Thirteen.)

Impotence is a tremendously common condition. Exactly how common nobody knows since so many sufferers hide their troubles away, believing that no-one can help them. But on any reasoned estimate the number of partly or completely impotent men in a country the size of Britain must run into millions.

But let me stress that an *occasional* episode of 'failure to perform' is of absolutely no significance. It's very common for normal healthy men to have a bit of difficulty in achieving a full erection now and then—when they're tired, or a bit over-eager (for example 'first night nerves' on honeymoon), or if they've had too much to drink, (the condition which is so succinctly termed 'brewer's droop'). Quite often, men to whom this happens for the first time in their lives decide that something awful has occurred (like the dentist in the film M*A*S*H who thought he was turning into a homosexual), but there's no need for such dire fears, *provided that it doesn't keep happening*.

But what if it does? Well, the important thing is to get treatment as soon as possible, before things get worse. Too often the husband becomes desperately embarrassed about what he regards as his 'failure', and he doesn't want to tell anybody about it. So he avoids sex altogether, hoping against hope that the trouble will go away.

The result may well be that his wife decides she is being scorned, and so needless bitterness arises between them. Alternatively, some women are cruel enough to sneer or laugh outright at an impotent man, which of course makes things 50 times worse for him.

What about remedies? As with other sexual problems, the basic idea of therapy is to let both parties talk about their problems with the doctor or counsellor and so come to realize *why* the trouble is happening. Many men improve as soon as they can be persuaded that they are not suffering from some horrible or permanent disease.

The wife must be taught that when her husband fails to get an erection she shouldn't just roll away in disgust, frustration or self-pity but that this is the time for her to metaphorically roll up her sleeves and get down to work on stimulating his penis (see Chapter Seven: *How to Handle a Man*). This is usually best done with the husband lying flat on his back and the wife sitting facing him, as in figure 47.

In this position, there is far less 'demand' on the man, and he can just lie back and enjoy being stimulated. When an impotent

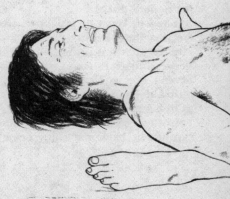

FIGURE 47

husband tries to make love in the 'missionary position' it is usually at the anxiety-provoking moment of 'climbing onto' his wife that he loses his erection.

As the man gets more confidence (and as his erection gets firmer) the wife can learn to move forward and 'mount' him, but as a rule this should *not* be attempted until the couple have been under treatment for several weeks. When the time comes to insert the penis, it's important that the woman should use her hand to steady it, and by gently supporting it at the moment of entry, she can help to prevent it from folding in the middle.

There is one other method of therapy that is available—desensitization treatment. Pioneered at St. Bartholomew's Hospital, London, this technique involves letting the patient relax on a couch and imagine the intercourse situation that he finds so frightening. Every time his anxiety starts to build up the doctor gives him a small dose of a sedative injection directly into an arm vein.

This treatment (which is also applicable to certain other sexual problems, such as vaginismus) produces improvement or cure in a majority of patients. If you are interested in having this therapy, talk to your GP about it in the first place, (but psychotherapy is often necessary as well).

Note: I have deliberately left physical causes of impotence to the end, as these are so rare. Diabetes may sometimes cause impotence, though we don't really know why. So may certain drugs, notably tablets for the treatment of high blood pressure. These drugs may also cause inability to ejaculate, that is, to produce seminal fluid at the end of intercourse. Changing to another type of tablet will usually result in a marked improvement.

Patients who have had really major abdominal operations (for example, removal of the bladder or large segments of the bowel) may sometimes become impotent because nerve tracts have had to be cut through. Where this is the case it is often wise to consult a specialist in urological surgery, who may prescribe a splint for the penis or even perform an operation to insert a plastic stiffening rod inside the organ.

PREMATURE EJACULATION. Also known as 'hairtrigger trouble', this is the very common condition in which the man cannot help reaching his climax too early. Quite often the disorder is associated with impotence, and the cause is the same—over-anxiety about sex. It's natural and inevitable that patients will try to deny this to themselves and to ascribe their trouble to being 'over-eager' or 'highly-sexed', but the truth is that as soon as the anxiety can be overcome, the patient will get better.

Many men (particularly young males, whose sexual apparatus tends to be somewhat explosively triggered) have discovered for themselves that one or two stiff drinks (*not* more, for fear of diminishing the potency) will sometimes take the edge off anxiety and so enable the climax to be delayed and intercourse to be prolonged. A mild tranquillizer an hour before bedtime can have the same effect, and some doctors have achieved good results by prescribing anti-depressant pills.

Patients with very mild premature ejaculation often find that they can successfully delay their climax by using what are called distraction techniques such as pinching themselves, biting the pillow, or thinking about football, fishing or the rising cost of living—in short, anything but sex! Other husbands seem to derive some benefit by applying a local anaesthetic ointment to the penis shortly before intercourse. These ointments can be bought at most sex aid shops.

However, a severely affected man is not likely to be helped by these methods. He requires the sort of psychotherapeutic discussion we have already mentioned in relation to other sex difficulties and this may often reveal that his early surreptitious sexual experiences conditioned him to reaching a climax as fast as possible. In addition to this both he and his wife need to be taught the technique invented by Dr. James Semans in 1956, and subsequently developed by Masters and Johnson.

I won't describe this technique in great detail here because it really requires the supervision of a skilled therapist but the general idea is shown in figure 47, which is based on the illustrations in Masters and Johnson's book *Human Sexual Inadequacy* published by Little, Brown & Co., Boston, Mass. and J. & A. Churchill, 15-17 Teviot Place, Edinburgh.

Basically the concept is for the couple to abandon intercourse altogether for some weeks. Instead they indulge in love play in the position shown, with the wife stimulating her husband's penis manually. Every time he warns her that he is about to reach a climax, she squeezes his penis very firmly (using the *exact* grip shown). Done properly, this immediately abolishes the desire to 'come'; the wife can begin stimulating again a few seconds later.

The discovery of this almost unbelievably simple technique can be said without exaggeration to have completely revolutionized the treatment of a disorder which had brought untold misery to countless marriages.

Summary

Some years ago a friend of mine got married for the second time and was appalled to find that he had become impotent. He went to his doctor who told him that this was the inevitable result of advancing age and that nothing could be done. I should add that my friend was then aged 39.

He was in deep despair for some days and, not surprisingly, practically gave up all hope of recovery as had been suggested. Fortunately, he then had the sense to go to his wife's GP who (like virtually all doctors) had had no training at all in sexual problems, but who was a kindly man with a good deal of commonsense. As a result of regular reassurance from this doctor over a period of several months my friend quite soon regained his potency. From then on he and his new wife were able to lead a happy and normal married life.

I don't for one moment blame the first doctor for the opinion he gave. It wasn't his fault that his medical school had never taught him anything about sexual difficulties. But the moral of this story is clear—if you have a problem with your sex life and you really want to get it cleared up, never, *never* give up at the first hurdle.

CHAPTER TWELVE
Trouble Down Below

Infections of the Sex Organs

Infections of the sex organs are very, very common indeed. These days, a young woman is probably more likely to get thrush or trichomonas (the two most frequent causes of vaginal discharge) than she is to get 'flu. Yet the astonishing thing is that very few women (or men) seem to know anything at all about these infections.

If you make love regularly (and sometimes even if you don't), you're very likely to acquire some sort of genital 'bug' at one time or another during your life, and this certainly applies to men as well as women, though men are fortunate in that the more trivial infections give them very little in the way of symptoms.

Happily, most of these disorders are not of any great consequence, *provided they're diagnosed and treated fairly rapidly.* So, whether you're male or female, I advise you to look through this chapter and get to know the warning signs of trouble down below; and if symptoms arise in you or your partner, do go and get treated by a doctor as soon as you can.

Thrush

Also known as Monilia or Candida, thrush is a fungus which infects human beings very frequently indeed. You can see what it looks like in figure 48(a). Babies get it in the mouth and adult women usually get it in the vagina, where it causes pain, soreness, itching and a thick, white discharge (rather like blobs of cottage cheese). The diagnosis is confirmed by taking a vaginal swab and examining it under a microscope. In men thrush may produce no symptoms at all or else slight to moderate soreness and redness of the penis.

Where does thrush come from? Well, obviously it can come from other people's sex organs (or occasionally their mouths), but

I hasten to add that if it suddenly attacks you this *doesn't* mean for one moment that your partner has been unfaithful! You see, a very high proportion of human beings go through life carrying thrush in their bowels. If you look at the diagram of female anatomy on page 41, you can see how very, very easy it is for bugs from the intestine to get across the couple of inches of skin that separates the back passage from the vulva, and this is probably what has happened in many cases of vaginal thrush.

A girl is more likely to have an attack of thrush if she's on the Pill; if she's recently had a course of antibiotics; if she's pregnant, or if she's diabetic. If you get *recurrent* vaginal thrush, it's best to have your urine checked for sugar, just in case. This also applies to men who keep getting thrush infection round the foreskin.

TREATMENT. Thrush can often be absolute hell for a woman, but treatment is very simple indeed, since a drug called nystatin

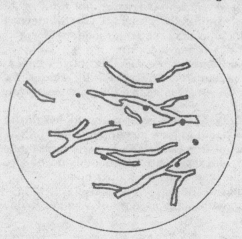

FIGURE 48a   *THRUSH*

produces virtually 100% cure if used properly though it often isn't, because people frequently give up the course too soon. Instructions for medication should always be followed exactly, right to the end of the course, even if the symptoms have disappeared.

I usually suggest to women with thrush that they insert a nystatin pessary (i.e. a vaginal tablet) every night and every morning for 14 days. Unfortunately, this is a bit messy, and it's often necessary to wear a pad for a day or two. Nystatin cream applied to the vulva (the outside of the vagina) is very soothing, and if the male partner applies it too it will eradicate any thrush lurking on his penis, whether or not he has any symptoms.

Many doctors also give their patients nystatin tablets to take by mouth, with the object of wiping out the 'reservoir' of thrush in the bowel, and this practice may be useful in delaying recurrences. However, I would stress that a lot of girls do go on getting thrush two or three times a year whatever therapy they have: this doesn't really matter as long as they get prompt and full treatment each and every time.

New preparations are becoming available which are rather less messy than nystatin pessaries and with some of these (e.g. clotrimazole or Canesten) it is often possible to eradicate infection in less than 14 days.

Finally, it's usual to advise anyone who has thrush not to have sex (or, at least, not to have actual intercourse) for at least a week after the start of treatment. This is a wise precaution, but in fact most women with thrush are so miserably uncomfortable that sex is about the furthest thing from their minds!

Trichomonas
The second most common cause of vaginal discharge is called

Trichomonas vaginalis. This is a bit of a cumbersome name, so the bug is often known as TV for short.

You can see what trichomonas (pronounced tri-ko-MON-ass) looks like in figure 48(b). There are literally millions of people (both men and women) going around with this tiny parasite in their bodies. Indeed, some investigators have suggested that as many as 23% of all women carry it, so it's not surprising that the infection it produces is one of the most common disorders of our time, though amazingly enough, even the name of the condition is still almost totally unknown to the public.

In women, trichomonas causes a very painful and irritating discharge. Usually, the fluid is yellowish or greenish and bubbly, and some women complain that it has an offensive smell. Characteristically, the opening of the vagina (the vulva) is bright red and so sore that intercourse is virtually an impossibility. The

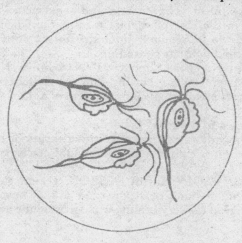

FIGURE 48b   TRICHOMONAS

diagnosis can be confirmed by taking a vaginal smear or sometimes by taking a cervical smear—a 'cytotest' just like the Pap smear for early detection of cancer of the cervix.

In men trichomonas may produce slight irritation within the urinary 'pipe', though most commonly the male partner of a woman with TV has no symptoms at all. <u>But he will very probably be carrying the bug without knowing it.</u>

This fact is very important, because it means that unless a girl's husband or boy friend is treated, he will keep on re-infecting her.

TREATMENT. Happily, treatment of trichomonas is pretty easy: both partners are usually given a course of metronidazole (Flagyl) tablets to take by mouth three times a day for about a week or so (longer courses may often be necessary). Flagyl can produce headaches and sickness, but these side-effects are unlikely to occur as long as the couple avoid alcohol during the period of treatment. They should also avoid actual intercourse, though (as in the case of vaginal thrush) the female partner is most unlikely to be remotely interested in sex until this painful and trying condition has cleared up.

Newer drugs such as nimorazole (Naxogin or Nulogyl) and nifuratel (Magmilor) are coming into use. Nimorazole has the advantage that it can be given in the form of a three dose 24 hour course.

Other Causes of Vaginal Disorders

Most women with a discharge have either thrush or trichomonas, but there are other causes of this symptom. Let's look at them one by one.

NORMAL VAGINAL SECRETION. I must stress that it's very common for younger girls to *think* that they have a discharge when they haven't. Every healthy woman has quite a considerable flow of vaginal secretion, the quantity of which varies from day to day and at various times of the menstrual 'month'.

The flow increases rapidly during sexual excitement, to provide lubrication for intercourse. And of course if that didn't happen love-making would be so difficult and painful for both sexes that the human race would have died out long ago. (A lady doctor who was lecturing a group of nurses expressed all this succinctly by saying 'Don't get your knickers in a twist just because you find some secretion on them, especially after a date.')

So, the presence of the 'love-juices' is just a sign that everything in your reproductive equipment is functioning normally. As long as the fluid is either clear or milky, there's nothing to worry about.

Don't be concerned about the slight aroma of vaginal secretion either. The love-juices do have a definite perfume, the biological function of which (though you may be surprised to hear it) is to attract and excite the male. Women don't usually like this fragrance very much, but it isn't meant to appeal to them.

Unfortunately, intensive advertising of vaginal deodorants has convinced a lot of girls that they oughtn't to smell of anything except *Joie* or Fragrance of Raspberries (there genuinely was a deodorant of this 'flavour', to quote the manufacturer's description).

These ideas are nonsense. If you want to go round with your pelvis smelling like the Perfumed Garden, good luck to you, but it certainly isn't essential to your health. And bear in mind that you could get a sensitivity reaction from the chemicals in vaginal deodorants.

Douching isn't necessary either. If you think you've got too much secretion, don't try to treat yourself, see a doctor for proper examination and investigation.

If you haven't got *enough* secretion, you should also see a doctor. Lack of secretion is a common cause of pain during intercourse after the change of life, and the use of a hormone cream will usually clear things up and restore love-making to normal. However, dryness of the vagina causing difficulty in love-making may also be due to emotional problems. Please see Chapter Eleven.

DISCHARGE CAUSED BY FOREIGN BODIES. After thrush and trichomonas perhaps the commonest cause of a real discharge in younger women is the presence of a foreign body, usually either a forgotten Tampax or a piece of tampon that has broken off. Objects introduced into the vagina while masturbating or during love play can also get temporarily lost and set up an irritation that causes a discharge. This is why popping things inside (a curiously widespread practice as I've already explained in Chapter Nine), is really extremely unwise.

DISCHARGE CAUSED BY DISORDERS OF THE CERVIX. All kinds of disorders of the neck of the womb (the cervix—see the picture on page 62, Chapter Two) may produce a discharge. The fluid tends in general to be 'catarrhal', 'slimy', brown or blood-stained.

If you get a brown or bloody discharge, it's *essential* that you are examined internally. The doctor may well be able to tell you exactly what's wrong simply by looking at the neck of the womb. Most often it will be a simple condition (like an erosion or a polyp) which a gynecologist can usually deal with (e.g. by cautery), without the necessity of admitting you to hospital.

DISCHARGE CAUSED BY GERMS. Vaginal discharge can be (and frequently is) due to the germs of gonorrhoea, a condition which we'll also deal with in this chapter.

Discharge may too be caused by bowel germs, and Masters

and Johnson have pointed out that where a discharge persists and where investigations by means of vaginal swabs is negative, the patient should be discreetly asked about her sexual hygiene. Often it will turn out that she and her husband are having first rectal and then vaginal intercourse, without washing between, which is very unwise indeed.

Gonorrhoea

This is a very, very common form of VD, frequently called 'clap', and its incidence has been rising rapidly in almost all Western countries since the 1950s. In Britain for example, it is now far more common than measles—though admittedly Britain's superb system of confidential VD clinics has kept the incidence much lower than in many other countries where gonorrhoea is practically reaching epidemic proportions. Indeed at the time of writing it has just been announced that there has been a slight, though alas probably temporary, fall in England's gonorrhoea figures.

This disease is caused by a tiny germ called the gonococcus. Like other forms of VD, it is to all intents and purposes acquired only by having some form of sex contact with an infected person. This need not amount to actual sexual intercourse, which is why —contrary to widespread belief—homosexuals very often get infected.

Someone having sex with an infected partner is not absolutely certain to catch the disease, but the probability of getting it is generally reckoned to be around 70%. The risk is reduced if the male wears a sheath.

In men, the symptoms are usually very clear cut. About two to four days after contact with a carrier of gonorrhoea, the man gets *a pus-like discharge* from his penis and finds that he has *severe burning pain on passing urine.* These symptoms are usually so un-pleasant that he will have the sense to go and have treatment, which is just as well, since the late complications of gonorrhoea are not much fun. They include joint troubles, eye inflammation, painful swelling of the testicles and distressing stricture (narrowing) of the urinary pipe.

Unfortunately, in women the early symptoms are far less definite. There may be pain on passing water and a vaginal discharge (usually yellow or green) but anything up to 50% of infected girls have no idea that anything is wrong until the disease is quite far advanced.

This 'hidden' gonorrhoea poses a very serious problem. Obviously, there must be thousands of women around who have no idea that they are incubating the disease, and many of these girls infect a number of men before their symptoms finally become apparent. By this time, a lot of harm may have been done to their reproductive organs. Gonorrhoea causes severe inflammation of the Fallopian tubes and ovaries,[1] the symptoms of which include lower abdominal pain, fever, menstrual irregularity and vaginal discharge.

Unfortunately, unlike *early* gonorrhoea (which is usually easy to treat), this kind of advanced gonorrhoea can sometimes respond very badly to therapy, and the girl may finish up sterile or in a state of chronic ill health. I have worked in a tropical city where the incidence of gonococcal infection was absolutely prodigious, and in the port area especially there were thousands of unfortunate women whose pelvic tissues had been almost destroyed by this cruel disease. I sincerely hope that most countries don't find themselves in the same boat in 20 years time.

TREATMENT. Happily, the unpleasant complications of

---

[1] *If you're not familiar with these terms, look at the picture on page* 62 *and read Chapter Two:* How a Woman is Made.

gonorrhoea need never occur *provided treatment is started early*. If you have symptoms that suggest gonorrhoea or if you have no symptoms but are just worried about the fact that you have had sex with somebody who might conceivably have been infected, then go straight to a VD clinic. You don't need a doctor's letter or an appointment, and all you have to do in order to find out the place and time of the clinic is to ring the nearest large hospital and ask where and when the next 'Special Clinic' is held.

The doctor at the clinic will do various tests and, if you prove to have gonorrhoea, he will simply give you an injection of penicillin, and ask you to come back later for further checks. Disregard those scare stories you've probably heard about having umbrella-like scraping devices pushed up the urinary passages. These instruments went out when penicillin came in many years ago.

In Britain, and in all areas where civilized standards of medical ethics prevail, absolutely no-one will be told about your case[1], not even your GP unless, of course, it was him who sent you along in the first place. People (and especially young people) often seem very suspicious about this question of confidentiality, and give false names (or even stay away from the clinic altogether) because they wrongly fear that the doctor is going to tell their parents, husbands or wives or employers. All I can say is that in Britain at least a venereologist who lost his reason sufficiently to do such a thing would rapidly find himself up before the General Medical Council.

So if you think you might possibly have gonorrhoea (or any other form of VD), please don't hide it away. Steer clear of sex until you've had your check-up, and get down to the clinic as fast as you can. Remember that if the infection is treated *early* it's certain to be cured.

---

[1] *This is not so in certain parts of the USA, where doctors are forced by State laws to disclose information about VD patients.*

NSU

These initials indicate not a make of German car but the condition called 'non-specific urethritis'. You've very probably never heard of NSU, but at the rate it's increasing you certainly will do in the future.

In Britain, NSU is now the commonest form of VD (more common even than gonorrhoea) and it seems certain that by the end of the century this will be one of the biggest health problems we're facing. Unless something remarkable happens it could well be that by that time the majority of young men will acquire NSU at some time or other—not a very cheerful or romantic-sounding prospect.

For NSU is really a disease suffered by males, rarely producing obvious symptoms in women, who are thought mainly to carry it. I would stress the word *thought* because we still know very little about what actually causes NSU. It's generally supposed to be a germ, but some venereologists feel that it might be a sensitivity reaction to thrush or some other factor in the partner's vagina. (I have recently read a popular magazine article which confidently states that NSU is 'caused by a virus': this may perfectly well be true but at present we have no proof whatever of it.)

At all events, NSU develops about a week or 10 days after having sex. The symptoms are very similar to those of gonorrhoea, but the discharge may persist for quite a long while despite treatment. Happily, serious complications of NSU are fairly uncommon, but the disease still needs treating as soon as possible.

TREATMENT. Tests are taken to rule out other forms of VD (especially gonorrhoea) and the patient is then given antibiotic tablets (usually tetracycline) to take by mouth. Repeat courses of tablets may be necessary, and follow-up visits to the clinic are always essential.

Syphilis

Syphilis is an appalling form of VD, caused by a germ called *Treponema pallidum*. Happily, the coming of penicillin back in the 1940s provided a complete cure for the disease, and it became very much less common after the Second World War.

Unfortunately, the incidence of syphilis has been rising very sharply in many parts of the world in recent years, though in Britain, and other countries with first class venereological services, it remains, thankfully, a rare disease.

So we'll deal with the symptoms of syphilis pretty briefly. Roughly a month or so after having some form of sex contact with an infected person, the patient develops what's called a *chancre* at the point of contact (most commonly, the penis or vagina, but sometimes the lip, nipple, finger, etc.). You can see what a chancre's like at its ulcerated stage in figure 49. Before ulcerating, it's a hard, painless sore, usually about the size of a fingernail. In a woman, it may be hidden deep within the vagina and therefore

FIGURE 49

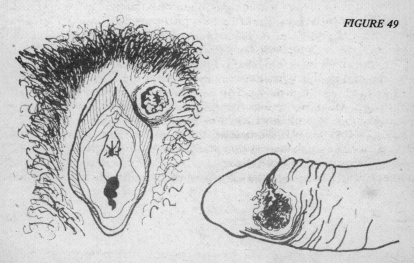

go completely unsuspected.

If the patient doesn't get treatment, the chancre goes away after a variable period, and the unfortunate person usually assumes that he's cured. This is the devilishness of syphilis, because he isn't.

Before very long, secondary syphilis will develop. This usually takes the form of a skin rash or an outbreak of mouth or throat ulcers. These symptoms too go away in time, but the germs may very well be still in the body and 12, 15 or even 20 years later they may drive the patient mad, cause him intense pain (tabes), paralyze him or destroy his heart and blood vessels.

Furthermore, any woman who has undetected syphilis will probably pass it on to her children, causing them terrible deformities, which is why routine blood tests for syphilis are done on all expectant mothers.

So, you can see that if untreated this disease is a pretty nasty customer. A savage old medical mnemonic runs:

> There was a young man of Bombay,
> Who thought syphilis just went away,
> So now he has tabes,
> And sabre-legged babies,
> And thinks he is Queen of the May.

Black humour perhaps—but the point is that syphilis doesn't just go away. Even though you don't seem to have any symptoms, if you have the remotest suspicion that you might have exposed yourself to the disease, and especially if you've had casual or commercial sex with someone, follow the advice given in the section on gonorrhoea and go straight to the nearest 'Special Clinic' for tests.

Happily, treatment for early syphilis, which is by means of a course of penicillin injections, invariably produces a complete cure.

Lice and scabies

Unfortunately, and unromantically, these infections are very frequently picked up during intercourse and through other forms of physical contact as well. Both types of infestation are becoming alarmingly common.

Pubic lice ('crabs') produce intense itching in the pubic hair. Before very long the patient can usually see the tiny crab-like creatures scuttling around, which is a pretty alarming experience. Scabies ('the itch') produces an even more intense irritation, which may be quite intolerable at night. It is much more generalized and affects most areas of the body, particularly the wrists and the 'webs' between the fingers. Characteristic little red bumps (which are the parasite's burrows) can be seen in the affected parts.

You can go to your own doctor or to a 'Special Clinic' for treatment, which is by means of a skin application, and as scabies in particular is exceptionally infectious, see your doctor or the Clinic as early as possible; avoid contact with others as much as you can, and use only your own towel.

Cystitis

Finally, a brief mention of cystitis. It's not strictly speaking an infection of the sex organs (the word 'cystitis' actually means inflammation of the bladder), but attacks of it are closely related to sexual activity and cystitis is quite uncommon in girls who are still virgins, hence the old name of 'honeymoon cystitis'.

The reason for this is quite simple. If you look at the drawing on page 41 (back in the chapter on female anatomy), you'll see that the distance between the urinary opening (the urethra) and the back passage (the anus) is very short indeed. Cystitis is usually caused by the common bowel germ (*E.coli*), which gets across the little space and finds its way up into the bladder. The germ can get across on sanitary towels, on the material of pants or as a result of lack of care in wiping the bottom after a bowel action[1]; but in practice it does seem that it is likeliest to be transferred during the rough-and-tumble of love-making.

You're probably well aware of the symptoms of cystitis— intense pain on passing water; having to rush to the lavatory very frequently; having to get up at night, and sometimes passing blood. Though these symptoms are very trying, many women regard cystitis as a pretty trivial complaint, but let me stress that it's *not*.

Doctors used to regard the condition as being as unimportant as a cold, and indeed many older physicians still take this view, but since the 1960s it has been generally felt that if cystitis isn't properly investigated and thoroughly treated there is a real risk of the infection leading on to kidney inflammation (pyelitis)[2], with the possibility of long term damage to the woman's health.

So I would recommend that if you get a bout of cystitis you should take a pain-killer, drink plenty of fluids and go to the doctor within 24 hours to ask him to send a mid-stream specimen of your urine (an MSU) to the local path. lab. From the result of this test, he'll be able to tell whether the antibiotic he is treating you with is the right one. Even though your symptoms go away, continue with your antibiotics for the full 10 or 14 days of the course and go back to the doctor for a check MSU in about a month to ensure that all germs have gone.

Finally, let me mention that there are quite a lot of women who get recurrent cystitis, but whose mid-stream urines show no bowel germs. Why this should be we just don't know. It could perhaps

---

[1]*Paediatricians say that little girls should always be taught to wipe* from front to back.
[2] *This subject is discussed fully in the preceding volume in this series,* The Home Doctor.

be that some of them have a *virus* infection of the bladder (which lab. tests wouldn't pick up), but most doctors think that cystitis symptoms are due to the recurrent trauma which love-making is bound to cause to the lower part of the bladder and to the urinary passage (the urethra). This may well be true in many cases of 'honeymoon cystitis', since both girl and boy are likely to be so nervous and unskilled that minor damage to the area of the urinary opening is almost inevitable. Finally, in some ladies these symptoms of cystitis do seem to be linked with emotional factors— in other words, they tend to get episodes of rushing to the loo when things are getting on their nerves (which is a fairly normal human reaction).

If you're one of those women who get recurrent cystitis but whose MSU tests don't show any germs, then it's best if you have a full investigation of your urinary tract, including x-rays, and that you seek gynecological advice, particularly about sexual hygiene (including the use of a bidet). You and your partner should wash carefully before beginning to make love. Applying a lubricant (such as KY jelly) before love-making may be helpful, and so may passing water immediately after intercourse, then washing carefully again. You may like to contact one of the clubs which have sprung up for recurrent cystitis sufferers—in England, contact the U & I Club, c/o 22 Gerrard Road, London, N.1.

The founder, Angela Kilmartin, has recently published a book called *Understanding Cystitis* which should help chronic sufferers.

CHAPTER THIRTEEN
Pregnancy and Sex

How to Get Pregnant

If you've read Chapter Three: *How Sex Leads to Babies*, you'll already have a pretty good idea of how to start a pregnancy. Basically, it's just a question of making love at the right time—in other words, the time of ovulation, which is when the ovum (egg) is released from the woman's ovary.

This is usually around 14 days before the start of a period. For a woman with a 26 day interval between her periods (which is pretty average) the likeliest time for conception to occur is therefore about the twelfth day of the cycle. You can see this in figure 11; note that as sperms can often survive for several days it may be well worth starting your attempt to get pregnant a day or two earlier, say, about the tenth or eleventh day of the cycle.

In fact, having completely unprotected intercourse most fertile couples will conceive within a matter of six to twelve months without even trying to concentrate on a particular time of the menstrual cycle, and some of them will 'hit the jackpot' the very first month.

What to Do if You Can't

INFERTILITY. There are a tremendous number of people who find it very difficult to start a baby. It's important to stress that the cause of the problem may well lie with the husband and not the wife. Even today, a lot of men simply refuse to recognise this fact and regard any suggestion that *they* should be investigated as an insult to their virility! This is very foolish, since the ability to have children is really nothing to do with one's prowess as a lover (some of the most frigid people on earth have six or ten offspring to their names). Furthermore, it's not a man's or a woman's *fault* that their fertility is below par—an affected person can't help it, any more than he or she can help having blue eyes or black hair.

If you've been trying to have a baby for somewhere between six to nine months and haven't succeeded then instead of struggling on alone do go to your doctor, who may well send you on to a gynecologist, or else go directly to a Family Planning Clinic. It's not generally realized that quite apart from birth control advice, these clinics do offer help to people with sex difficulties and sub-fertility problems.

EXAMINATION AND ADVICE. The first thing that the doctor will do is to examine you, just to make sure that no structural abnormality is present. (Ideally, he should see both the husband and the wife.) In the vast majority of cases, he'll be able to reassure the couple that there's nothing anatomically wrong, though a proportion of wives may require treatment to some slight problem of the cervix or neck of the womb, such as an erosion.

It's also important to ensure that the husband and wife really are having intercourse. I know that sounds extraordinary, but the fact is that a proportion of all the wives who come to subfertility clinics turn out to be still virgins. Such is the sad state of sex education (even in this allegedly permissive society) that many of these couples don't even know that they haven't been doing the right thing to make babies.

Indeed, I have even heard of a case in which a doctor's wife who was being investigated for infertility was found to be a virgin. The puzzled doctor eventually decided that ever since their marriage they had actually been having rectal and not vaginal intercourse—which is perhaps a rather horrifying comment on the state of sexual education in our medical schools.

Once it has been established that the couple are having normal intercourse, the next thing is to enquire whether the husband is actually reaching a climax. In some cases of infertility the real problem is that the man is having trouble with his potency and is not in fact having an orgasm. Let me stress, however, that it doesn't matter a bit for conception to take place whether the wife has a climax or not. Any number of women seem to have the idea that it's their 'frigidity' that's preventing them from conceiving, but this isn't true at all. If you're a wife who has trouble reaching a climax then read Chapter Eleven: *Problems with Sex*—but bear in mind that this difficulty definitely won't stop you from having a baby. I always remind patients who think that a female climax is necessary for conception that any number of unfortunate women have conceived as a result of being raped.

POSITION OF LOVE-MAKING. Thanks to the researches of Masters and Johnson, it has become apparent in recent years that when a couple are having trouble starting a baby, the position in which they make love does make a bit of difference. The average woman's womb points forwards and the neck of her womb (her cervix) points backwards. As you can see from the picture on page 65 (Chapter Three), this means that her cervix will dip into the pool of seminal fluid that has been squirted out by her husband *only if she lies flat in the 'missionary' position*. Conception will be aided if she stays in this position for about 15 minutes after intercourse, preferably with her bottom on a pillow and her knees raised.

But a considerable minority of women have a cervix that points forward. When he examines you, ask the doctor if this applies in your case. If so, then your best chance of conception will be to make love in a kneeling position, like the one in the picture on page 142 (Chapter Nine). The wife should stay in this position for a quarter of an hour after intercourse, but the husband can get up and go and make her a cup of tea. After 15 minutes she'll probably need it!

TEMPERATURE CHARTS. Next, the doctor will ensure that you're making love at *approximately* the right time of the month, as we've discussed at the beginning of this chapter. I say 'approximately' because this method of just selecting the 'middle of the month' (or 14 days before a period) is not very accurate. A lot of wives defy Nature by ovulating at other times of the month, which is why the famous 'Rhythm and Blues' method is so risky (see Chapter Ten: *How to Prevent Babies*).

So, for more precise measurement what we do is to put the wife on a daily temperature chart. You can see a typical example in figure 50. Note that the woman has taken her temperature every morning and recorded it on the graph. The doctor's instructions on how long to leave the thermometer in the mouth and so on must be followed to the letter.

Now on this particular graph, the wife's temperature has gone along pretty steadily until the eleventh day after the start of her period, when it fell slightly to 97.4°F (36.3°C). On the following day, it 'kicked' upwards to 98.6°F (37.0°C), and it is this 'kick' which indicates probable ovulation taking place. (It's important for the wife to record factors—like colds—which might have caused a slight elevation of temperature; you can see that this patient's thermometer reading went up slightly when she got a cold shortly before her next period.)

In fact, one month's recordings aren't much use since by the time you know ovulation has occurred, it's already almost too late! But after six months or so on a chart, the couple will usually know fairly accurately when ovulation is likely to be expected. Obviously, on that particular day (and more particularly on the

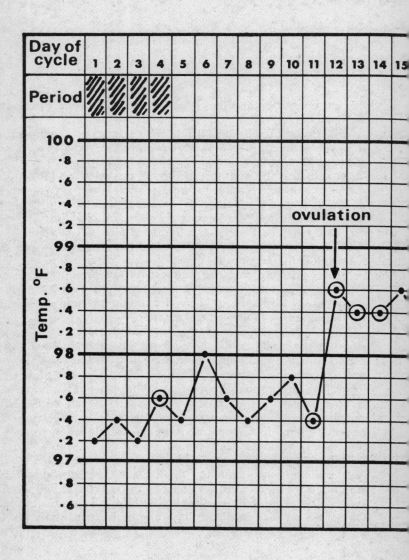

FIGURE 50

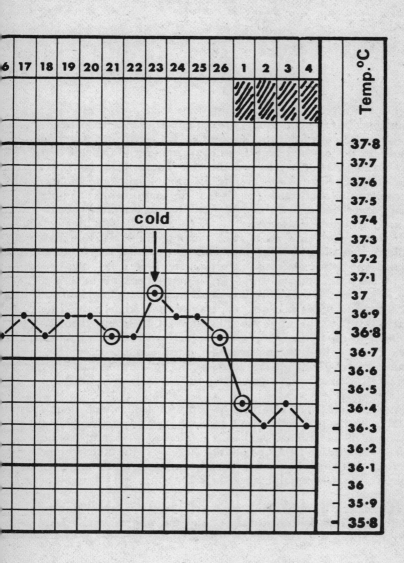

night or two preceding) they must 'seize their opportunity with both hands', as a lady doctor of my acquaintance tells her patients.

As you can see from the illustration, it's usual to put a ring round the dot on the temperature chart in order to indicate that love-making has occurred, and the aim should really be to get four or five circles in a row around the time of ovulation. In fact, a temperature chart often reveals that the main reason a couple aren't conceiving is that they just aren't having sex often enough to make it statistically likely.

If there is no 'kick' on a wife's temperature chart, this may indicate that she isn't ovulating, so further tests will have to be carried out by a gynecologist. Fortunately, even if it is the case that she is not producing eggs (ova), it may be possible to correct this by giving the wife a 'fertility drug' to stimulate her ovaries.

SPERM COUNTS. If her temperature chart seems to indicate that she is ovulating, but she still can't get pregnant, then it's essential to do a sperm count on the husband. Indeed, it often saves time to check this at an earlier stage in the proceedings— I have known husbands feel so reassured at knowing that they were 'OK' that they have gone home and got their wives pregnant straight away!

A sperm test is nowhere near as bad as it sounds, and there's nothing for the man to be afraid of. All he has to do is provide a specimen of his seminal fluid in a clean jar, so that it can be looked at under a microscope (*not* urine or any of the other strange offerings that embarrassed men sometimes bring in). A sample in a sheath is not acceptable since the rubber may kill off many of the sperms.

This means that the fluid can't actually be collected during intercourse, but there's no reason why the wife shouldn't help the man to obtain it during the course of love play, if he doesn't feel like obeying the usual rather bleak and clinical instructions to 'provide a fresh masturbation specimen'. The fluid should go to the lab within an hour or so, and is best kept in the pocket on the way there so that it remains fairly near body temperature.

I must stress that only labs which are experienced in doing sperm counts should carry out this sort of work. One of Britain's leading experts in this field recently said that many of the sperm reports he saw were absolutely useless, because a lot of technicians as yet don't really know how to do the tests. In other words, don't take your sperm count along for checking at your local cottage hospital, since the results are likely to be unreliable.

If the husband's sperm count is rather low, it's sometimes possible to do something about it by dealing with any minor anatomical abnormality, for instance varicoeles (which are varicose veins just above the testicle). Attempts are also being made to treat subfertile males with new fertility drugs, though this work is in the early stages as yet.

Much more important is the simple manoeuvre of *keeping the testicles cool*. This sounds slightly ludicrous, but the fact is that if the male sex glands are kept at a highish temperature, then the sperm count tends to go down.

There have been cases of long distance lorry drivers who had trouble getting their wives pregnant and who succeeded only when they took a break from work—the reason being that if you sit on a plastic seat in the sweltering heat of a lorry cab for eight hours a day, your testicles are practically bound to get overheated.

Most husbands with a lowish sperm count are not long distance lorry drivers, however, and the manoeuvre that is of most help to these men is simply to stop wearing jockey-type shorts (which keep the heat in around the scrotum), and to change to loose shorts. Unfortunately, jockey shorts have acquired a very masculine image in recent years, and it is sometimes difficult to persuade men to switch to garments which they regard as slightly effeminate. One doctor working in this field gets round the problem by always describing the looser, cooler pants as 'boxer shorts'.

OTHER TESTS. There are other tests which are useful in helping a couple to have a baby, but a detailed description is outside the scope of this book. They include the post-coital test, in which the wife is examined internally some hours after lovemaking, to see how well the husband's sperms are able to survive inside her body; endometrial biopsy, in which the gynecologist scrapes a little tissue from the inside of the womb for examination under the microscope, and tubal patency testing. This last procedure involves taking the patient into hospital to examine her (usually under anaesthetic) and to determine whether there is any blockage in the Fallopian tubes.[1] If there is, it may be possible to clear it surgically, and indeed experiments are going on with implantation procedures that would bypass the Fallopian tubes altogether.

ARTIFICIAL INSEMINATION. Sometimes it may be necessary to perform artificial insemination, either with the husband's own sperms (AIH) or, if he doesn't appear to be producing any of his own, with sperms from a donor (AID).

AIH causes few problems, and most couples are delighted with the results. AID is a more complex business, however, and it is essential that the husband and wife are properly counselled by a specialist in this field and that they make sure that they both really do want the wife to bear another man's child before they

---

[1]*See Chapter Two:* How a Woman is Made.

go ahead. Where this is what the couple sincerely want, the results are very good indeed.

All that is necessary is for the wife to go along to see the specialist at the approximate time of her ovulation. He will inject some seminal fluid (taken from a donor who is completely unknown to the couple) into the upper end of her vagina. It's often advised that the couple should make love within 24 hours or so, so that they will be able to feel that there is at least some possibility that the child might be the husband's. If this is done, he need have no qualms about registering the baby as his own.

Love-making during Pregnancy

Once you've conceived there's usually no reason why you should not go on enjoying love-making throughout pregnancy. A lot of people still seem to have the wrong idea about this and one comes across wives (and indeed husbands) who, because of sexual hang-ups, arbitrarily decide that it would be 'best' to avoid intercourse for the whole nine months. Some of them then wonder why their spouses go off and seek consolation elsewhere.

In fact, there are very few circumstances in which a couple would have to stop love-making because the wife is pregnant. The safest rule is to check with your GP or your obstetrician if you happen to run into any difficulties with the pregnancy. In particular, cease love-making if any vaginal bleeding occurs, and don't resume till you get a go-ahead from the doctor. Incidentally, don't be afraid to ask him. The days have long gone when it was considered 'not nice' for people to raise these topics in the consulting room.

What about if you have been trying hard to have a baby and have had miscarriages in the past? Here I think it definitely is better to take things a bit easy in the early months, and to be guided entirely by the doctor's advice.

It's traditional to say that any pregnant woman who has had miscarriages in the past should avoid intercourse at the times when her period would have been due. I don't know of any firm evidence for this belief, but there may be some truth in it and it's certainly no hardship for a couple to avoid these particular times, at least for the first five months.

LATE PREGNANCY. What about at the end of pregnancy? Until quite recently, many doctors and midwives used to advise against sex during the last couple of months before baby was born, but as long as all is going well (and your obstetrician has no objection) it should be safe to indulge in *gentle* love-making at this time. (Obviously no-one but an idiot would go in for rough and violent wooing.) Indeed, I even know one obstetrician who advises expectant mothers who are a few days overdue to go home and gently make love to see if this will start things off.

POSITIONS IN PREGNANCY. After about the fourth or fifth month, love-making in any of the male-superior positions (such as the traditional 'missionary' position) tends to become very uncomfortable for the wife. So it's usually much more pleasant to make love in positions where the husband's weight isn't on the wife's body.

Particularly useful are any of the rear entry methods shown in Chapter Eight, plus any of the female-superior ways of making love described in the same chapter. Also very nice is the side-entry (or flank) position illustrated in Chapter Eight, in which, as you can see, the wife lies on her back so that there's no strain on her tummy at all; her husband lies beside her, with his thighs curled up under her bottom.

In fact, for many couples, pregnancy is the time when they

first find out about new and enjoyable alternatives to the more orthodox positions.

LOVE PLAY IN PREGNANCY. However, there *are* times when intercourse simply isn't practical for a pregnant woman, particularly if there is some obstetric problem such as recent vaginal bleeding.

But in these circumstances, there's no reason at all why a couple who enjoy sex should give up enjoying the warmth and tenderness of mutual physical love. Though intercourse may be out, the man and woman can of course continue to excite and satisfy each other with love play as outlined in Chapter Six: *How to Handle a Woman* and Chapter Seven: *How to Handle a Man.*

I recently read a very good article by a nurse who cheerfully said that 'pregnancy is a wonderful time for inventing perversions'. I wouldn't use the word 'perversions' myself, but it's quite true that pregnancy often is the time when a couple really begin to discover how much fun it can be to excite each other with caresses of the fingertips, lips and tongue. Because the wife's breasts tend to be particularly full and generous at this time, exciting the husband's penis between her breasts (as shown in figure 17) may be especially nice for both of them.

One note of caution about oral sex. It's quite all right for a pregnant wife to bring her husband to his climax by placing his penis in her mouth, but in the later part of pregnancy, say, from the sixth month onward, it is best if she takes care not to swallow any of the fluid he produces. (As we've explained in Chapter Seven, the majority of wives don't like swallowing the fluid, but quite a lot of women do.) It has recently been pointed out that there is a possibility that a woman whose pregnancy was nearing its end could be put into premature labour by ingesting the chemicals called 'prostaglandins' which are present in the man's seminal fluid.

Indeed, as I explained back in Chapter Nine, the world's leading authority on prostaglandins has said that his original research into these remarkable chemicals was sparked off by hearing that among certain African tribes a woman whose labour was overdue was often 'induced' by giving her a somewhat unappetizing-sounding draught of her own husband's semen in water.

Sex Problems in Pregnancy

Though most couples immensely enjoy love-making in pregnancy, there are others who find that things suddenly start going badly wrong when the wife is expecting. She may perhaps become unresponsive when she knows that she is pregnant or (more commonly) when she first feels the child move within her. Similarly, (though much less frequently) the man may start having troubles with his potency when his wife conceives.

These difficulties may be partly related to unnecessary fears about injuring the baby in the womb, but it's more likely that they are connected with long-standing sexual hang-ups. Thus a wife may feel deep down that it's quite OK for people who aren't parents to enjoy sex, but that all this should be over and done with when she is about to become a mother. The identification with her own mother (who is thought of as disapproving of sex) is fairly obvious.

A very similar phenomenon very often occurs when a woman who is unsure of her sexuality gets married and then suddenly becomes frigid. Subconsciously, she feels that climaxes were all right for a girl indulging in a spot of premarital fun, but not for a respectable married woman!

If you run into sexual difficulties during pregnancy, first have a look at Chapter Eleven : *Problems with Sex*, and then seek professional help. Since an antenatal clinic isn't usually the best place to spend half an hour or so discussing your sex life, it may be best to take your spouse along to your local Family Planning Clinic. Your expectant mum's tummy may look a bit odd in these surroundings, but the doctors will still be very pleased to see you.

Love-making after Childbirth

There's a rather indelicate medical joke which runs : 'Doctor, doctor, how soon after delivery can I make love to my wife?' 'Ah—that depends whether she is in a private or a public ward!'

This attitude strikes me as overdoing things slightly. However, there's no doubt that in days gone by fearful couples used to postpone the resumption of love-making far longer than was necessary—for six months or a year in some cases.

The simplest thing is to ask your doctor or midwife how soon intercourse can be resumed. If there has been no damage to the vagina it's usually quite alright to start again within a matter of a couple of weeks or so, but if you've had stitches the obstetrician may well advise you to wait until after the post-natal check-up, which is usually done when the baby is about six weeks old.

If you get any pain during intercourse always tell the doctor and get him to examine you. As I hope I've made clear in Chapter Eleven : *Problems with Sex*, pain in the vagina during love-making (particularly in younger women) is usually due to tension, but after childbirth it may well be caused by infection or a tender scar.

Indeed, I have even seen a wife who came up to a gynecology clinic nine months after delivery to complain that she had had persistent pain on intercourse ever since. Examination revealed that the poor woman still had a thick black suture (stitch) across the lower half of her vagina. A quick snip with the scissors restored that particular couple's lovemaking to normal.

Contraception after Pregnancy

I look forward to the day when every woman who has just had a baby will be offered family planning advice in the ward. Remember that <u>many mothers get pregnant again even before their first period has arrived</u>, so do please start taking contraceptive precautions (even if it's only the sheath and pessary method as described in Chapter Ten) as soon as you come out of hospital, even if you're breast-feeding. If you wish, you can have an IUD (coil, loop) fitted before you leave the ward—indeed, insertion is easiest at this time. Or, if you've completed your family (and if you give the obstetrician plenty of warning of your intentions), he may well be willing to sterilize you while you're still in hospital.

Some doctors are not keen to put wives on the Pill until their periods have begun again, but others are quite happy to do so as long as she is not breast feeding. However, many doctors are willing to prescribe the 'Mini-Pill' for a mother who is still feeding her baby herself.

All these methods of family limitation are fully dealt with in Chapter Ten : *How to Prevent Babies.*

CHAPTER FOURTEEN
Abortion

Failure of Contraception

Almost every abortion could have been avoided by contraception. To put it at its mildest, it's a great shame that so many single girls and married women end up having terminations these days. In England, for example, at the present time, at least one pregnancy in every eight is terminated.

Frankly, it's all so unnecessary—if you use a sensible method of contraception (see Chapter Ten: *How to Prevent Babies*), the chances of starting an unwanted pregnancy are pretty slim. Yet even people like nurses, teachers and women doctors (all of whom might have been expected to know better) continue to have to go through the upsetting experience of having a termination, just because they (*and* their husbands or boy friends) haven't had the sense to go to a Family Planning Clinic or to a doctor who gives contraceptive advice. It's a crazy world.

The only cheerful thing about the present position is that, contrary to what so many self-appointed moralists tell us, the majority of women who have abortions do learn by their mistakes. Only about 2% of them are unfortunate enough to have a second termination, which I think refutes the argument of those who claim that 'it's all too easy for these flighty young girls to go and have abortion after abortion these days'. In point of fact, only about half of all terminations are carried out on single girls; almost as many are performed on respectable married women who for one reason or another cannot cope with any more children.

So most people do learn to use contraception after the termination of an unwanted pregnancy. I only hope that one day we get to the situation where everyone (both male and female) has the sense to use it beforehand.

Illegal Abortion

Deliberate abortion was almost always carried out illegally until quite recently. This meant that it became the province of the criminal back street operator, usually an unqualified person with little or no knowledge of hygiene. There are still many such people around and not just in countries where termination is still forbidden by law, but in areas where expense and other factors (such as unwillingness of local gynecologists to do abortions) make it difficult for less well-off women to obtain a legal termination.

Let me stress as strongly as I can that no pregnant woman should ever consider going to one of these back street abortionists, no matter how bad things may seem. I don't say that criminal abortionists are necessarily wicked people (for doubtless some of them are genuinely trying to help girls in distress), but their clumsy, untrained efforts with their unsterile instruments have killed many a woman in the past.

Far more frequently, however, their crude gropings will cause intense pain, heavy blood loss and serious infection of the sex organs. The woman who goes to this kind of practitioner may have her health crippled or become sterile. Although some people certainly do escape unscathed from the unqualified abortionist's hands, I would say that the majority run into some sort of trouble. In the days before legalized abortion, one could walk into the gynecology ward in any large hospital and practically guarantee to find someone recovering from the consequences of an illegal abortion attempt. (In England, the number of septic abortions dropped by nearly 60% in the first three years after the passing of the Abortion Act.)

It goes almost without saying that attempts at self abortion are just as dangerous as back street terminations. Women still buy all sorts of preparations from the chemists and take them by mouth or place them in the vagina. These methods are most unlikely to get rid of the baby, but they may well seriously harm the mother.

Therefore if you genuinely want a termination, get one done legally by a competent and reputable surgeon. This chapter will tell you how to go about it.

Legal Abortion

THE LAW. Since the late 1960s, a number of countries (and American states) have introduced laws that allow doctors to perform therapeutic termination of pregnancy. The situation varies greatly in different areas, however. Legal abortion is permissible in Great Britain but not yet in Northern Ireland, and in New York State but not in many other parts of the USA. It seems likely that more and more countries which at present forbid abortion will in due course bring in more liberal laws based on the British/New York state pattern, though there are obviously great difficulties in framing any kind of ideal legislation.

In countries where therapeutic abortion is allowed, the law contains certain safeguards intended firstly to make sure that demands for termination are not made frivolously, and secondly to protect the expectant mother. Unfortunately there are all too many thugs and shady characters who are ready to exploit a woman's distress for money, and indeed one of the more un-pleasant consequences of the liberalization of abortion laws has been the fact that a good many touts and businessmen (and even a few doctors) have seen the new situation as their chance to get rich.

So, if you have decided that you definitely want a termination, do go to a reputable doctor (preferably your own GP in the first place), and he will ensure that the requirements of the law are complied with.

PROCEDURE. The important thing to stress is that if you think you are pregnant, you *must* act with considerable speed. Don't wait about for several months hoping that things will 'put themselves right'. By that time a termination may be difficult or even impossible.

When your period is 12 to 14 days overdue, have a urinary pregnancy test performed. Your own doctor (or the doctor at a Family Planning Clinic) can arrange for the specimen to go to your local hospital's path. lab, but if you really don't want to consult him at this stage you can go to any large pharmacy where pregnancy testing is offered. Alternatively, you can send the specimen of urine to one of the commercial pregnancy testing services which advertise so widely these days. Bear in mind though that one or two fly-by-night operators have entered this field, so that results should be interpreted with caution. Indeed, no pregnancy test is 100% certain, which is one reason why you really need a doctor's advice right from the start.

In any case, if your test is positive you will now *have* to consult a doctor who will assess whether you're eligible for termination. While I think it's desirable for you to see your own GP (who probably knows your home and health background), you are not obliged to do so and you can of course consult any doctor who is willing to see you. If in doubt, contact one of the charitable (not profit-making) pregnancy services, who will arrange for you to be seen by one of their doctors. If you can't pay the fees, they will lend you or even give you the money.

Warning: Beware of 'advice services' whose purpose is to extract the maximum amount of money from you. Reputable charitable organizations are not very likely to make contact with you through airport touts or taxi drivers or even through commercial pregnancy testing services.

The doctor whom you consult has to decide, on the basis of your reasons for wanting a termination, whether it would be justifiable to recommend one. The law varies from country to country, but in Great Britain the essence of the Abortion Act is that the doctor must feel that to continue the pregnancy would pose a greater threat to the mother's health (physical or psychological) than if she had an abortion.

In fact, it can be shown that it is actually *safer* to have an early termination than it is to have a baby, and a surprisingly large number of British doctors now interpret the Abortion Act in this light. In other words, though they will carefully counsel a woman who asks for a termination, and even try and persuade her against it, nonetheless they will recommend it if she sincerely and genuinely wants it.

At the close of the interview, the doctor should tell you whether or not he will recommend a termination. If he won't do so, then you should seek advice from another physician as soon as possible, and certainly within a week. If you are determined to have a termination, it should be possible to find a reputable doctor who will refer you to a sympathetic gynecologist.

But above all, <u>don't delay.</u> It becomes more difficult to terminate pregnancies when more than 12 weeks or so have elapsed since the start of the last period, and six weeks will already have passed by the time you know you are pregnant.

THE OPERATION. Once you have legally been 'accepted' for a termination, you'll be given a date on which to attend the hospital or licensed clinic, and you'll be told what sort of operation will be done.

Early pregnancy. If no more than about 12 weeks have elapsed since your last period, it will be relatively easy to terminate the pregnancy by the vaginal route. There are two main methods of doing this—by scraping the womb, and by vacuum aspiration.

A 'scrape' of the womb is simply the well-known 'D & C' (dilatation and curettage) procedure. You go into the hospital or clinic several hours (at least) before the operation, and you're carefully examined by a doctor to see if you're fit for a general anesthetic. Then you're given a pre-med injection and prepared for theatre. Finally you're put to sleep (usually by means of an injection in the back of the hand), and when you wake up 15 minutes or so later, it's all over.

While you were asleep, the gynecologist passed an instrument through your vagina and through the little canal that runs through your cervix (the neck of the womb), in order to scrape the interior of the womb itself. If you don't understand the anatomy of all this, then look at the picture on page 62 and read Chapter Two : *How a Woman is Made.*

You may feel a bit low after the 'scrape', but in any case you must remain in the hospital or clinic overnight. (If a clinic wants to turn you out because they need the bed, threaten to report them.)

Vacuum aspiration came into widespread use in the early 1970s, and is now more commonly employed than the traditional 'scrape'. Often you don't need to have a general anesthetic and all that happens is that the gynecologist inserts a suction catheter through the neck of your womb and sucks out the contents. Recovery is usually quick, and though I think the current term that the newspapers apply to this method (the 'lunchtime abortion') is perhaps a bit misleading, the doctor may well agree to letting you go home without spending the night in hospital if your period is only about 2-4 weeks overdue. However, do read the section on Aftercare later in this chapter.

Later in pregnancy. Ideally, every woman who is going to have a termination should have it done by about the twelfth week, since after that time the operation is more difficult and the risks increase. (If you are paying for it yourself, the costs are probably going to be higher too.)

The traditional way of terminating a pregnancy at this later stage is by making an incision in the abdomen and cutting the womb open (just as in a Caesarian operation). In the case of a woman verging on middle age, actual removal of the womb (hysterectomy) may sometimes be done instead. Because these are abdominal operations, the patient has to stay in hospital much longer. In Great Britain, at the time of writing, I'm sorry to say that about one termination in 18 is still done by the abdominal route. A lot of women could be saved a lot of trouble and complications if they were operated on earlier by the safer and easier vaginal route.

Other methods of terminating women who reach the gynecologist too late for a 'scrape' or a vacuum aspiration include the injection of salt or other solutions into the womb, usually through the abdomen but sometimes via the vagina. In very skilled hands, these techniques give quite good results, but the incidence of side-effects is still much, much higher than with vaginal termination in early pregnancy.

Some gynecologists also use infusions ('drip' injections into an arm vein) of chemicals which will make the uterus contract, and one particular group of these chemicals (the prostaglandins) can be injected directly into the womb. This method has given promising results but it is not yet in very widespread use.

Aftercare

If, like the vast majority of patients, you've had an ordinary vaginal termination (either by a scrape or by vacuum aspiration) then you'll probably be back in normal health within a matter of a few days. But do take the gynecologist's advice about how soon you should resume housework, physical exercise and love-making. And bear in mind that complications such as infection and bleeding can occur; if you start running a temperature, or if you develop a discharge or heavy blood loss or abdominal pain, seek medical help right away.

After an abdominal termination even more care is necessary, but the surgeon will advise you about this. It's not usually wise to resume any kind of work (including housework) for several weeks.

But perhaps one of the most important aspects of aftercare is making sure you don't get pregnant again. Ideally, your doctor or the gynecologist should raise this matter with you, but if they don't, then ask them. It's possible to fit an IUD (loop, coil, etc.) at the end of the operation — or indeed to have a sterilization carried out if you've completed your family. As soon as you come out of hospital, you can begin taking the Pill or have a cap fitted. Alternatively, you could persuade your husband or boy friend to use a sheath. Some husbands will decide to go and have a vasectomy because their wives have gone through a termination, if the family is completed. All these methods of family limitation are discussed in Chapter Ten : *How to Prevent Babies*.

At all costs, don't subject yourself to the trauma of having another unwanted pregnancy, because this is quite likely to be damaging psychologically as well as physically.

Furthermore, there's quite a lot of evidence that termination (and particularly repeated termination) can damage the neck of the womb and thus cause problems (such as miscarriage and premature birth) in subsequent pregnancies. So if you haven't yet settled down and started a family, it's especially important that you don't have any more abortions. Even if when you come out of hospital you swear that you'll never run the risk of getting pregnant again, it could be a very good idea to go and get some family planning advice. Remember that many of the 2% of women who do have repeat abortions thought exactly the same as you.

Menstrual Extraction ('Overdue Treatment' or 'Interception')

In the early 1970s, a new method of fertility control became popular in the USA and by 1974 its use was becoming quite widespread in many other countries. The basic principle of the method is very similar to that of vacuum aspiration abortion (see the earlier part of this chapter) in that a slim catheter is slipped through the vagina and into the womb in order to suck out its contents. The procedure is usually fairly painless and takes only a couple of minutes.

Doctors who use this method say that it should be employed not when the patient already knows she is pregnant but before she has even missed a period, perhaps even the morning after intercourse. They prefer to regard the technique as 'bringing on a period' rather than as an abortion (since very frequently indeed, the woman isn't actually pregnant anyway).

They therefore refer to the method as 'menstrual extraction' and dislike the popular term 'overdue treatment'. Indeed, using this technique when a patient was actually overdue with her period would certainly amount to carrying out an abortion in the eyes of the law at present.

Supporters of menstrual extraction say that it will become the sort of procedure that GPs can carry out in their surgeries for women who come in saying that they have had unprotected intercourse and want their periods brought on. This may well be so (judging by the popularity of the method in America), but I do feel it would be a great deal more sensible if people used contraception in the first place, rather than waiting till the morning after.

The 'Morning After' Pill

While on the same subject, let me just say that there is a 'morning after' pill (which is nothing to do with *the* Pill, i.e. the oral contraceptive). The idea is that a woman who has had unprotected intercourse can be given very high doses of an oestrogen (usually stilboestrol) for several days afterwards, with the idea of aborting any pregnancy which may be forming.

I don't personally think that this treatment is a very good idea. Firstly, the high doses involved often produce intensely unpleasant nausea and vomiting. Secondly, most of the girls who take the treatment aren't pregnant anyway, so they are subjecting themselves to these side-effects for nothing. Thirdly, the method isn't 100% effective, so that unless a follow-up abortion is available, a number of women are going to go on carrying babies who have been exposed to massive doses of stilboestrol during their first few days of life in the womb.

Does the last point matter? Yes, it does. One of the greatest medical tragedies of this century was the administration of much lower doses of stilboestrol than this to pregnant mothers in an attempt to prevent recurring miscarriages. Fifteen or 20 years later, the daughters of some of these women suddenly started developing cancer of the vagina—a horrifying indictment of the kind of biological time-bomb that man can set ticking when he starts playing around with hormones whose long-term effects he doesn't really understand.

In short, where pregnancy is concerned prevention really is better (and safer) than cure. It's a lot more sensible to take contraceptive precautions before making love than to be desperately scurrying around trying to do something about it afterwards. However, in absolute emergency (e.g. following a rape) it is certainly worth while trying to put things right the morning after unprotected sex. In such circumstances, your doctor may well be willing to prescribe a high-dose Mini-Pill to be taken either in single or in double dosage for about 10 days.

CHAPTER FIFTEEN
A Final Note

Of necessity, the last few chapters of this book have been mainly about the less glamorous aspects of love—abortion, infertility, infections, sexual problems and so on.

But love is meant to be a cheerful and joyous business. It's sometimes hard to remember that fact in these days when people take sex so very seriously. At times, it seems as if the world is divided between those guilt-ridden Clean-Up-Everything campaigners (who treat sex as if it were a dangerous animal that has to be muzzled, if not actually put down) and those terribly intense sexual liberationists (who seem to be hell-bent on some sort of erotic revolution in which the entire population, from eight to 80, would be expected to take part in daily orgies).

I don't think the rest of us, who constitute the vast majority, should be swayed too much either way by these serious-minded

gentry, whether they're the stern puritans who still want the human race to equate 'sex' with 'sin', or the slide-rule sexologists who seem to think we should all be fulfilling a quota of 10 partners a day.

After all, sex is *fun*—so let's keep it that way. There are far, far too many people who try to turn the whole subject into something sober, grey, straight-laced and calculating. But love should not be like that at all. It's a wonderful, spontaneous, marvellous exciting and beautiful thing—the warmest, most comforting and nicest sensation on Earth. Love brings happiness, joy, tenderness and (perhaps above all) *laughter* into a world that would otherwise be sadly barren of these commodities. May everyone who reads this book enjoy it for many a long, long year to come.